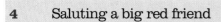
A **BUSES** MAGAZINE SPECIAL PUBLICATION

# CONTENTS

(PW), Tony Wilson (TW)
**Advertising manager:** Sam Clark
**CEO & Publisher:** Adrian Cox
**Commercial Director:** Ann Saundry
**Marketing Manager:** Martin Steele
**Group Editor – Transport:** Roger Mortimer

www.keypublishing.com
www.busesmag.com

**Printing:** Precision Colour Printing Ltd, Haldane, Halesfield 1, Telford, Shropshire, TF7 4QQ
**ISBN:** 978 191 2205 42 4
**Registered office:** Key Publishing Ltd, Units 1-4 Gwash Way Industrial Estate, Ryhall Road, Stamford, PE9 1XP

**Fifty years ago, London Transport tried replacing many of its double-deckers with high capacity single-deckers like AEC Merlin MB641 as part of its bus reshaping plan (see p82).** TERRY BLACKMAN

Cover: **London Transport RTL453, a 1949 Park Royal-bodied Leyland Titan PD2 preserved in the Ensignbus heritage fleet.** KEITH McGILLIVRAY

# Saluting a **big red** friend

***As recognisable abroad as Big Ben or pillar boxes, the red London double-decker remains a great British icon. One that has evolved through years of triumph and adversity***

Along with red telephone boxes and pillar boxes, black taxis, Big Ben and police officers in helmets, the red London double-decker remains one of the most instantly recognisable images of Britain today, identifiable internationally and often used to emphasise the Britishness of exports.

In this publication, we salute the 9,500 buses — nearly three quarters of them are double-deckers — in service across London today, a fleet that has grown in 50 years from around 6,000 to meet the complex travel needs of a population that continues to grow. This is one of the most intensive public bus services in any city in the world.

We also salute the London buses of past decades, the tens of thousands of them that have served Londoners and those visiting London since before London Transport — forerunner of today's Transport for London — was created in 1933.

We tell their story partly through significant anniversaries reached in 2018. Seventy years

ago, in 1948, London Transport had just been taken into state ownership and was already embarking on the most intensive investment in new buses seen anywhere in Britain, as around 7,000 new vehicles poured into its fleet over a period of just seven years.

Not just any buses, but vehicles built to London Transport's own exacting standards. These were standards of mechanical refinement based on its own operational experience, and of aesthetic and practical design inspired by the organisation's prewar determination that its vehicles and buildings should be visually appealing as well as being fit for the job they were expected to do.

## The RT family
By far the most numerous of these new buses were the AEC Regents and Leyland Titans that formed the RT family of double-deckers. A standard design that could be operated almost anywhere in London and overhauled on a production line basis at the large engineering works that London Transport

built to support its fleet.

These buses were needed in order to replace old vehicles kept running longer than intended after war broke out. They were needed to complete a programme begun in 1935 to replace London's trams with buses. And they were needed to replace the utilitarian buses — non-standard vehicles — that had come during and immediately after the war.

Many of these older vehicles were fit only for scrap, but London Transport did find new homes for its wartime utility buses, nearly 200 of them with prominent operators in Scotland who recognised their potential and transformed many of them into what most passengers could assume were new vehicles.

Ten years on, in 1958, things were looking a lot less promising. London's population was falling and with it the number of people riding on its bus services. Not just non-standard wartime buses were being sold out of service, but the last of the new RTs spent years in storage before going into service, while some of the earlier ones were disposed of as surplus to its new requirements.

Worse still, labour relations were deteriorating, prompting an all-out strike by bus crews that spring, a stoppage that lasted seven weeks, discouraged even more people from riding by bus and led to some major cuts in the number of routes that were operated. It would take well over 40 years before passenger numbers got back to where they were before that strike.

Another 10 years and, in 1968, London Transport was implementing its bus reshaping plan, a brave attempt to tackle the woes that had beset it since the mid-1950s.

This was a turning point in the design of the London bus. The RT had paved the way for the ultimate development of its traditional double-decker with engine alongside the driver and conductor on an open platform at the back, the Routemaster. The first one appeared in 1954 and production got under way from 1959, enabling this legendary vehicle to replace the large fleet of electric trolleybuses operated mainly in north and east London.

The last of 2,760 Routemasters arrived in early 1968, but although a prototype with a rear engine and front entrance was on trial, this was the end of the bespoke London double-decker. Or at least for the next 40 years.

It looked even as if this could be the end of the London double-decker, as the reshaping plan embraced ideas from overseas in the shape of single-deckers in which many passengers would be expected to stand at busy times. Like they did on the Underground or commuter trains.

It also looked like being the rapid end for the bus conductor, too, as the new buses — operating shorter routes in many places — would only have a driver. Passengers would either pay the driver or use one of the fancy self-service machines available to pay a fare and perhaps receive a ticket.

The plan got off to a roaring start in 1968, but the new buses came with all sorts of faults and unexpected operational complications and were soon considered such a mistake that many were put up for sale with the same haste that had cleared out those wartime utility buses 20 years earlier. The red double-decker refused to go away and was back in fashion. Universal driver-only operation would have to wait for advances in electronics and payment systems that even science fiction writers would have struggled to predict over 40 years ago.

New vehicles came and went and the Routemaster — the last traditional London double-decker — went on and on, upgraded mechanically and refurbished inside, until the last few hundred were finally retired in 2005.

## On the up again

By then the London bus was on the up again, with many services running round the clock and the network carrying increasing numbers as the population also kept on rising.

There was a brief flirtation with high-capacity single-deckers on some of the busiest routes, articulated vehicles better known as bendybuses, but a change of mayor saw them shipped off as peremptorily as the products of the bus reshaping plan or those wartime utility buses.

Back came a red double-decker designed exclusively for London, a hybrid electric with three doors, two staircases and — briefly — the facility to hop on and off the backs of some of them when they were held up between stops or were waiting at red traffic lights. An internationally esteemed designer was given the task of making them look stylish. And they were given a name. New Routemaster.

Today there are 1,000 of them among the 9,500 London buses, along with a few other double-deckers with styling features taken from this design. But there will be no more, it seems, as another mayor has come along with his own priorities for public that include cheaper fares and no more New Routemasters.

Another priority is to clean up London's air quality. Buses are in the forefront, with ultra-low emissions — even zero emissions where possible — the base requirement for central London, ultimately beyond. Buses will also be removed from Oxford Street in the heart of the West End.

The number of electric and hydrogen-fuelled buses is growing and the technology of the ever larger fleet of hybrids continues to advance.

This is a story that is continuing to evolve and in this publication we pause to consider some of the major parts of it, as well as looking at some of the buses around London today, the routes that they ply and the garages that support them.● **AM**

**BELOW: Film extras pose as London Transport driver, inspector and conductress against a line of four RTs in the Ensignbus depot.** KEITH McGILLIVRAY

# The legend that was the RT

ABOVE: RTL22
and an early
postwar RT at
Victoria Station.
This is how these
buses looked
when new, with
cream paintwork
around the top
deck windows and
with a reduced
destination display
to conserve stocks
of the material
used to produce
destination
blinds. One of
the Bristol Ks on
loan from Tilling
Group companies
is alongside.
MICHAEL H. C. BAKER
COLLECTION

*The RT family of nearly 7,000 double-deckers was the most numerous London double-decker ever produced, most of them built around 70 years ago, between 1947 and 1954, to replace a worn-out fleet of older vehicles and to oust the last double-deck trams*

The long awaited arrival into service of the first postwar RT on 10 May 1947 heralded an extraordinary seven-and-a-half year period, culminating in November 1954, with the replacement of virtually the entire fleet of London Transport's prewar and wartime buses and coaches and the remaining prewar trams by 7,000 vehicles, almost all of a virtually standard design of double- and single-deckers.

Nothing like it had ever happened on such a scale in such a relatively short period of time before in London, nor probably in any other great city, and probably will never happen again like it did 70 years ago.

As a result of the war, buses

which had an intended lifespan of 10 years had to soldier on, the oldest having their lives almost doubled, despite the fact that during the war maintenance was drastically reduced.

During the war, London was allocated 556 double-deckers built to wartime specifications. Although in most cases the chassis and engines were of a reasonable standard, the basic bodies used unseasoned wood framing which deteriorated rapidly so that London Transport was as keen to remove these from their fleet as it was the worn out prewar vehicles.

Forty-three trolleybuses destined for South Africa were diverted to London during the war and put to work in the Ilford area. Trolleybuses — electric vehicles drawing their power

from overhead wires the length of their routes — had been replacing trams in a planned manner since 1935 and if the war had not intervened the last tram would have quit the streets of London in 1943.

Although 77 new Q1-class trolleybuses arrived in 1947 and 1950, it was announced in November 1946 that diesel buses would replace the remaining trams and, eventually, the entire trolleybus fleet, which at the time was the largest in the world.

## Cutting edge?

Impressive as it was, by 1947 the RT — a variant of AEC's Regent III — was hardly at the cutting edge of the latest technology. The chassis of RT1 had been completed nine years earlier and after trials with a body from a

1932 Leyland Titan, its proper, intended body was completed in April 1939 and RT1 made its first public appearance in July.

Almost immediately 150 more RTs were ordered, followed that November by an order for a further 338. Although the original 150 all entered service, the last did not do so until February 1942 and the 338 had to be cancelled for the time being. When production eventually resumed after the war, there were modifications to the original design but nothing of great significance.

By the end of 1947, 171 new RTs had entered service. As a 10-year-old bus spotter, I became aware, and was much excited, by their arrival, on account of the fact that our local garage, Croydon, had received 39 of them for routes 115, 130 and 197.

I saw these beautiful new buses every day, for the 115 passed the end of our road. It struck me then, and it still does, how odd this choice was, for all three routes were extremely suburban, none getting anywhere central London. The remainder of the 1947 arrivals did work in and out of central London, from Leyton, Loughton and Potters Bar garages.

The official explanation was that the oldest, petrol-engined buses, in Croydon's case former Tilling and London General ST and STL-class AEC Regents, regardless of the routes they operated, went first, along with open staircase and other six-wheel LT-class AEC Renowns from the north London garages.

Throughout 1947 and beyond, hundreds of buses were being condemned by Ministry of Transport inspectors every month. The situation remained critical. Prewar, London Transport had built most of its bus bodies at its own Chiswick Works, but it was now fully occupied with chassis work, and from the start of postwar production the Park Royal and Weymann companies, both with

**ABOVE: The wider RTW class remained in service until 1966, when RTW170 was photographed in Thornton Heath on the long 109 route, which for many years linked Victoria Embankment and Purley through south London districts from Kennington, Brixton and Streatham to Croydon.**

**RIGHT: One of the first RTs delivered with the route number display alongside the destination and via screens was Park Royal-bodied RT928, new in November 1948.**

factories in the London area, were contracted as bodybuilders.

But even working flat out, neither company could totally satisfy London Transport's needs, so two other firms,

Saunders of Beaumaris in Anglesey and Cravens of Sheffield, were contracted to build 250 and 120 bodies respectively.

AEC, boasting the proud motto

Builders of London Buses and with its factory in Southall, had worked closely with the Chiswick engineers on the design of the RT, but its main rival, Lancashire-based Leyland, over

**ABOVE: RTs and RTLs replaced London Transport's remaining tram routes by 1952. Here, an RTL follows a tram on route 40, which linked Victoria Embankment and Abbey Wood along the Old Kent Road.**
GRENVILLE WILLIAMS

the years had also provided buses and trolleybuses for London.

It was asked to supply 1,000 modified Titan PD2 chassis — the RTL class — on which the RT body could also be fitted, plus 500 8ft wide chassis complete with Leyland's own bodies — the RTW class — which Leyland agreed to make as close to the standard RT body as possible. Metro-Cammell of Birmingham, a partner of Weymann in a joint sales organisation, built 450 bodies on RTL chassis.

All this took time, the first RTL entering service from Sidcup garage in December 1948, the first RTW in May 1949.

## Begging and borrowing

In the meantime things were only getting worse, with vast numbers of worn out buses being declared no longer roadworthy. A desperate solution to a desperate problem resulted in local coach operators being approached and the first of around 350 coaches started work in October 1947.

Wildly unsuitable for Central Area bus work, few having more than 31 seats and none more than 35, but better than nothing, they came with their own drivers and London Transport conductors. They were employed mostly, but not exclusively, on rush hour work. A few former London Transport buses and coaches also returned, briefly, to the fold.

Quite the most unexpected apparition was of 190 brand new Eastern Coach Works-bodied Bristol K type double-deckers. London Transport Executive, replacing the London Passenger Transport Board in 1948, was part of the state-owned British Transport Commission, as was the Tilling Group, which operated buses across England, Wales and south-west Scotland.

Tilling was directed to send 25% of the double-deckers it had on order to London. Tough luck on operators such as Hants & Dorset, Eastern National and Crosville, which were expecting them.

Most were of lowbridge layout, a clumsy arrangement with seats upstairs arranged in benches of four reached from a sunken gangway running the outside length of the bus. That got the Metropolitan Police highly bothered and it was reluctantly persuaded to allow their use on a few approved routes.

All the Bristols eventually reached their rightful owners by June 1950. There were also a few other double-deckers on loan.

Another emergency stopgap was the SRT class. These were refurbished STL chassis fitted with brand new RT bodies, which were ready before there were new RT chassis to accommodate them. They were introduced in February 1949, but proved to be underpowered for their heavier new bodies and had inadequate braking. All were withdrawn by July 1954, the bodies then being refurbished, repainted and fitted to new RT chassis.

## Regular rides

In September 1948 I became a pupil at Whitgift Middle School in Croydon and was initiated into the roughhouse mysteries of rugby football at the school's playing fields at Shirley. To begin with, this meant a ride in an Elmers End-based six-wheel LT, but within a couple of weeks these veterans were replaced by sparkling new RTs.

These, however, were no ordinary RTs, or at least not what we had become used to as the norm, for on the newest the number box had slid down from the roof and was now to be found alongside the via box at the front of the upper deck. This was revolutionary indeed (although it had been a feature of many prewar STLs) and we eagerly jotted down their numbers, beginning with RT860.

Shortly afterwards, in February and March 1949, Croydon garage received a run of 16 such buses,

**RIGHT:** The first of the Leyland-built RTLs to arrive, in 1948, was Park Royal-bodied RTL501. That was because the original plan was to number the RTWs and RTLs in a common series, but it was then decided that there would be RTLs from 1 to 500 and one of those, RTL68, stands to the right of RTL501 in this picture taken at Sidcup garage.
MICHAEL H. C. BAKER COLLECTION

**RIGHT:** An RTL crossing Tower Bridge. RT793 made headlines here in December 1952 when the bridge began to open as the route 78 double-decker was crossing it. The driver accelerated and the bus leaped across the widening gap without falling into the River Thames.

RT1136 to RT1148, and these instantly became my favourite RTs.

Logically, there is no reason why one particular group of buses should be any more favoured than any other out of 4,825 more or less identical ones, but such are the ways of bus spotters.

Not that they were really identical, but we will come to that in a minute. Inside the RT, and this is what counts, it was a masterpiece of design and there was a smell like nectar – perhaps I exaggerate slightly – a combination of the Rexine-covered seats and fresh paint. To quote the London Transport Museum, the RT featured 'advanced streamlining, bright interior, comfortable seating, smooth new diesel engine, air brakes and a preselector gearbox'.

The town of Croydon was also served by green London Transport buses from seven Country Area garages. The first green RTs went into service in July 1948, north of the river, at Tring garage. A month later, Leatherhead in Surrey received its first RTs and these soon appeared in Croydon. One of the first batch of green RTs, RT604, was still at work with what had become London Country Bus Services, part of the National Bus Company, at Chelsham garage in 1978.

To be strictly accurate and make no false claims, the overhaul system that London Transport employed meant that a bus that emerged after overhaul possessed neither the same body nor the same chassis as when it went in. Only the number was the same and not the bus. That utterly confused us bus spotters and a lot of other innocent bystanders too.

## Different designs

By now, production of new RTs, RTLs and RTWs was in full flood. It was a wonder to behold. By the end of 1949, 2,518 had arrived.

Although in a sense the 4,825 RTs produced were of a standard design, as were the 1,631 RTLs and the 500 RTWs, there were many variations, particularly concerning the bodywork.

The 120 Cravens RTs departed farthest from the norm, being essentially of that company's standard, with five window bays instead of four, although internally the difference was less marked.

I mentioned that the position of the number indicator came down from the roof in late 1948, but production of buses with this feature nevertheless continued, on Cravens and Saunders RTs, the last of the latter, RT4267,

**LEFT: Green London Transport Country Area RT2119, new in 1949, operating one of the longer routes out of Croydon.**

not arriving from North Wales until February 1951. Such a high number for a bus of what was now an antiquated design was because the various builders were allocated numbers in blocks.

Two visual variations that considerably altered the look took place in 1950. With the introduction of spray painting in the spring of that year, instead of having cream around the top deck windows, buses became either red or green all over, the only relief being a cream band between the upper and lower decks, which looked okay when brand new, but soon took on a rather dull aspect. Colourful advertisements all over the bus improved things.

Then in the autumn the full destination blind display, abandoned during the war years, was at last restored.

In that year, the astonishing total of 1,828 new buses entered service, the greatest number of new buses ever introduced in London in one year, before or since. Not only were prewar and wartime buses being replaced, but the final withdrawal of trams began on the night of 30 September/1 October.

The last new RTW took up work in December. The Metropolitan Police was wary of allowing 8ft wide buses into central London, but was convinced after trials and these

500 Leylands became a feature of some of the busiest routes serving the City and West End.

Thirty-six of the new RTs were painted in Green Line livery and put to work out of Romford garage on the intensive 721 and 722 services, replacing wartime Daimler double-deckers and prewar STL Regents. Internally they were to pure bus specification, but they looked smart.

## Delivery is completed

Another 873 new buses were put into service in 1951 and 655 in 1952, which also saw the complete elimination of trams from London, and 602 in 1953. Production of the RT and RTL ended in 1954, the very last, RT4794, arriving in November, although the highest numbered, RT4825, arrived in March. RTL1631, the last of the new Leylands, arrived in November.

The halcyon days were already over. Patrol rationing had ended in May 1950, car sales really took off, although for many young men and women their first car was a prewar Austin Seven. There was less demand for public transport, particularly in the evenings as people preferred to watch television rather than venture out to the cinema, and 63 new RTLs and 81 RTs went straight into store.

The following year withdrawal

of the non-standard Cravens-bodied RTs began, these still excellent vehicles being snapped up for many years' service with new owners all over Britain. Then in 1957 standard postwar ones began to be withdrawn, the oldest registered ones first, even though this meant that the bodies might be only four years old.

The 151 original RTs ended passenger service in May 1955, except for a brief foray into the Country Area by seven in 1956/57. Gradually the stored RTs and RTLs entered service in the place of their withdrawn, older fellows, the very last — green RTs — taking up work in the summer of 1959. Many of them appeared in Croydon, initially without advertisements and, while not quite sparkling after five years in store, were still a fine sight.

In order to complete the story, I must mention the lowbridge double-deck fleet, which was still needed and consisted of 76 RLH-class Weymann-bodied AEC Regent IIIs of purely provincial design delivered in 1950 and 1952, 715 AEC Regal IV single-deckers (class RF and RFW) plus 84 GS-class 26-seat Guys delivered between 1951 and 1953, but the story of those single-deckers must be left for another The London Bus in another year. ● **MHCB**

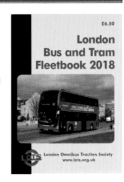

# The 1958 bus strike

## A bitter pay dispute took most of London Transport's buses off the streets for over six weeks in the spring of 1958, leading to a big drop in the number of passengers using the service and consequent cuts in services and the early disposal of many vehicles

BELOW: One of the buses operated by The People's League for the Defence of Freedom during the strike, a 1939 Northern Counties-bodied six-wheel AEC Renown still in the livery of original owner Leicester Corporation, heading south across Tower Bridge in June 1958. The warehouses of St Katharine's Dock are behind, buildings transformed today into fashionable housing, shops and restaurants.

BOTTOM RIGHT: Another casualty was route 17 between Shepherds Bush and London Bridge, on which RT916 appears here with an RTL behind. Later in the year this RT received a rear-end shunt, as a result of which the body was rebuilt with a right-hand platform and left-hand stairs as a sales vehicle for potential overseas buyers, by now mounted on the chassis of RTL3. It was last heard of 50 years ago somewhere in the area of Geneva.

Like most of the UK, London Transport emerged from World War 2 in not too great a shape.

As Michael Baker explains in his article about the 1947-54 investment in new buses, the postwar imperative was to renew the bus and trolleybus fleets while scrapping the remnants of the tram system.

Unfortunately, London Transport based its vehicle orders on immediate postwar passenger statistics, and seemed not to have the foresight to perceive a gradual recovery and ensuing prosperity, as a result of which it underestimated declining passenger levels and over ordered on its vehicle requirements. Hence 144 new RT and RTL double-deckers going straight into store, stripped of their tyres and wheels.

Economic recovery also had an impact on the labour market and, with the benefit of hindsight, arguably the nascent rumblings of discontent at London Transport became apparent in August 1957, when the Transport & General Workers Union submitted a claim for an increase of 25 shillings per week (£1.25p in decimal currency, or £29.75 at today's values) for all bus workers that it represented

across Central Buses, Country Buses and the Green Line coach operations; this covered all bus crews and some engineering staff.

London Transport, chaired from 1953 to 1959 by senior railwayman Sir John Elliot, rejected the claim totally and recommended that it be referred to arbitration. The union's general secretary, Frank Cousins, rejected that suggestion equally vociferously.

It looked like stalemate. Nevertheless, the two sides began further talks on 28 December 1957. Before this, in the autumn of 1957, London Transport had proposed draconian cuts to route schedules, which the TWGU scuppered.

However, the summer

programme introduced on 30 April 1958 included a majority of the cuts intended in the previous autumn's schedules, but as a red rag to a bull provocation, London Transport indicated that these cuts were only the tip of the iceberg and that more, equally severe, cuts

were to follow.

Adding fuel to the fire was a decision to convert 65 RF-class AEC Regal IV single-deckers to one-man operation. With all of the claims and refusals being passed to and fro, the TGWU requested that all be referred for arbitration by the Industrial Court, to which London Transport agreed, albeit grudgingly.

## Pay claim rejected

On 11 March 1958 and in response to all of the aggro, the court put forward a suggestion of an increase of 8/6d (42.5p, or £9.78 today), but limited solely to Central Area drivers and conductors. The argument of

the union was that the increase should be awarded to all staff represented by the TGWU; the response by Sir John Elliot was that as the union had proposed arbitration, it was incumbent upon it to abide by the decision of the court.

Frank Cousins's answer to that was to lodge a fresh claim of 10/6d (52.5p, or £12.08 today) for all staff, and without

**ABOVE: The lowest numbered of the routes withdrawn in August 1958 following the strike was the 4A on which RTL770, with Metro-Cammell body, was photographed preparing to leave Finsbury Park station for Camberwell Green. A trolleybus stands behind.**

**RIGHT:** Probably as a result of the post-strike cuts, in November 1958 was withdrawn from Southall and Uxbridge garages the last of the sub-class 14T12, 1946-built AEC Regal II single-deckers with Weymann bodies. This is T744 at Haven Green, Ealing, a vehicle sold the following month to the Ceylon Transport Board, which bought many surplus London Transport vehicles.

resolution of this, on 2 April informed London Transport of the union's decision to withdraw all labour on 4 May, as endorsed by a majority of the 100-plus delegates representing the TGWU staff employed at all garages and the Aldenham and Chiswick overhaul works.

London Transport treated this with hardly-disguised disdain, and both sides became entrenched in their attitudes.

By the end of April, London Transport granted that crews working the double-deck Green Line routes from Romford and Grays garages should be included in the arbitration award. As a result, the TGWU reduced its claim to 6/6d (32.5p, or £7.48), but reaffirmed that the revised figure must apply to all staff. The reply from London Transport was a predictable thumbs down.

Bloody-mindedness by both parties ensured that the strike went ahead, starting on 5 May 1958, and made certain that all road services were withdrawn — Central Buses, Country Buses, Green Line, Private Hire and Sightseeing — with pickets placed at all facilities covered by the TGWU.

While both sides were playing from a poor deck, the union delegates had overlooked a significant item, the London railway system.

Both British Railways' and London Transport's Underground employees were represented by the National

Union of Railwaymen (NUR), which declined the invitation to support its TGWU brothers.

Virtually all main line termini were served by one or more Underground line and those that were not invariably were within walking distance of one. Additionally, there was a comprehensive suburban system provided by British Railways, particularly in south London and the outer suburbs in Berkshire, Buckinghamshire, Essex, Hertfordshire, Kent and Surrey, thus the bus strike was never ever going to be 100% effective, thereby taking much of the wind out of the TGWU's sails.

### Fleet changes

While the dispute was brewing, the two Leyland-powered Routemaster prototypes went into service in January 1958, CRL4 from High Wycombe garage on Green Line route 711 from 8 January and RML3 from Willesden on route 8 from 22 January.

Released from store the next month were the final RTs and RTLs stockpiled since 1954, the operation being completed in March. All entered service with unpainted wheeltrims and without any exterior advertising.

This permitted the disposal of older RTs and RTLs in an apparently illogical and haphazard manner. This plan took no heed of the Aldenham overhaul system whereby, for example, a bus could enter the works as a 1949 chassis with a 1953 body and fleetnumber RT4237 and emerge as RT205 with a 1954 chassis and 1954 body. Thus were sold many low-numbered buses that had not even been built in 1947 and which were relatively new, say only three or four years old. That situation prevailed for most of 1958 until somebody in the organisation realised what was going on.

During the strike, and in revenue service for a little over two months, Clay Hall-based RTL1581 was burnt out beyond repair in what were described at the time as 'mysterious circumstances'.

Arguably the most interesting development during the strike was the granting by London Transport of a short-term licence for the operation of seven bus routes by The People's League for the Defence of Freedom, one of whose founders described himself as an 'independent right-wing' former Liberal. The routes included one in central London and six in various suburbs; it used a mix of secondhand vehicles provided by a dealer based in south London.

After negotiations, the strike was called off on 19 June and services resumed two days later. Central Area drivers and conductors were paid the extra 8/6d proposed by the Industrial Court, while all other grades received five shillings (25p, or £5.75 today).

As in many industrial disputes, there were no winners, possibly the worst affected being London Transport. While pre-strike staff shortages totalled 10%, the strike had exacerbated this situation, with many bus workers leaving the organisation's employ.

### Routes are withdrawn

Such was the aftermath of the strike that 20 Central Area routes were withdrawn completely in August 1958, resulting in the withdrawal of 175 RT, RTL and lowbridge RLH double-deckers on weekdays, 125 on Saturdays and 18 of them on Sundays.

Further cuts in the November involved complete or partial revisions to 33 more Central Area routes, while cuts caught up with the trolleybus system on 9 January 1959 when routes 664, 683 and 695 were culled.

Three garages, Clapham (converted to a bus garage only eight years earlier), Putney Bridge and Old Kent Road, were closed.

Strike-bound passengers had found alternative means of travel and passenger loadings dropped alarmingly, taking around 50 years to recover. ● **MJD**

# Route 13

I t is rare for a London bus route to be lengthened these days; when change does come, it usually involves a curtailment aimed at improving timekeeping. The 13 is an exception to this pattern. In 2017 it was extended northwards by three-and-a-half miles from Golders Green to North Finchley.

However, it wasn't the first time this had happened. In the 1930s the northern terminus was Hendon. It was cut back to Golders Green in 1952, but in 1978 it was extended northwards again, this time to North Finchley. That arrangement lasted for 15 years, then it was cut back to Golders Green once again. So now history has repeated itself.

There have also been changes

at the southern end of the route. The southbound 13 used to run along Oxford Street between Orchard Street and Regent Street, then make its way down to Piccadilly Circus, Trafalgar Square and the Strand, ending up at the Aldwych. Until 1970 it continued into the City, terminating at London Bridge.

In 2017 it was one of the first routes to be removed from Oxford Street as a result of Mayor Sadiq Khan's drive to ban all buses from the street (more about this on p36). Rather than improvise a new way to reach the Aldwych, Transport for London diverted the route down Park Lane and Grosvenor Place to Victoria, cutting perhaps half a mile off the overall distance.

This meant that the route was now identical to the existing 82, which was therefore withdrawn (or merged with the 13, as TfL puts it). At the same time 24hr operation was introduced. The 13 is now a high profile, high-intensity trunk service, with buses leaving as often as every 5min. At peak times the 10mile route requires around 30 buses.

For many years Routemasters were used on the 13. A notable landmark came in 1993 when BTS Coaches won the contract to operate the route, becoming one

of the first two private companies in London to operate the type. The company and its successors (ultimately London United) held on to the route in various guises for nearly 25 years, though the Routemasters disappeared in October 2005. The 13 was, however, one of the last routes to use them. Only the 38 and 159 kept them longer.

Coinciding with the latest route changes, the contract to run the route was won by Tower Transit, which is using a new batch of Volvo B5LH hybrid double-deckers with MCV EvoSeti bodies built in Egypt. I found these comfortable and remarkably quiet, though I wasn't impressed by the very thick inclined front window pillars on the upper deck. They didn't prevent me from enjoying the often striking views, but I feel they are a regrettable design feature.

Starting alongside Victoria station, the 13 makes its way northwards via Grosvenor Place, passing the Buckingham Palace grounds on the right. Continuing round the Hyde Park Corner one-way system, it heads up Park Lane, passing hotels and millionaires' apartments on the way to Marble Arch.

It runs briefly east here on Oxford Street, using a short stretch that will be spared the mayor's pedestrianisation plans. Then it's a left turn into Portman Street, which merges into Gloucester Place, running parallel to Baker Street. Historically these two roads have formed matching sides of a north-south one-way system, but as I prepared this article plans were afoot to reduce them in width and convert them both to two-way running in a radical attempt at traffic calming.

The southbound journey, incidentally, passes some notable landmarks on Baker Street. The office block at number 55 was home to Marks & Spencer for 100 years, but has recently been refurbished in dramatic style as a business centre. M&S moved to Paddington in 2004.

**BELOW: Tower Transit MV38201, one of the MCV EvoSeti-bodied Volvos built for route 13, approaching Lord's on a northbound journey.**

**LEFT: The thick window pillars viewed from inside the top-deck.**

North of Marylebone Road is the modern-style office block that was once the Abbey National building society's headquarters. Its range of street numbers (219–229) takes in the fictitious home of Sherlock Holmes, 221b, though this part of the street had not been built when Conan Doyle's books were written.

After the inevitable queue to cross Marylebone Road, we continue north past Georgian terraces into elegant and leafy Park Street, which runs along the western side of Regent's

**LEFT: A northbound 13 in the fast moving traffic that characterises the dual carriageway Park Lane along the north-eastern edge of Hyde Park.**

**LEFT: Marks & Spencer's store on the corner on the corner of Oxford Street and Orchard Street, passed by southbound buses on the 13.**

**ABOVE: The dramatically redeveloped business centre at 55 Baker Street, site of the former Marks & Spencer headquarters.**

**ABOVE RIGHT: The former Abbey House in Baker Street, built over the fictional home of Sherlock Holmes.**

**MIDDLE RIGHT: MV38231 passes St John's Wood Church, built 204 years ago.**

**BOTTOM RIGHT: The London Central Mosque in Regent's Park.**

Park. The minaret and golden dome of the London Central Mosque gleam out from the greenery.

The top of the road is dominated by the pillared 1814 St John's Wood Church, and in the centre of the roundabout in front of it is a bronze World War 1 memorial depicting St George slaying the dragon. Curiously, this is a 1935 casting of a statue that was designed by Charles Leonard Hartwell in 1923. The original stands in Eldon Square, Newcastle upon Tyne.

Following the road round the chicane into Wellington Place, we pass Lord's Cricket Ground, whose sleek Media Centre pod seems to hover over the site like an errant spaceship. It was the world's first semi-monocoque aluminium building, and won architectural prizes when opened in 1999, despite the dramatic contrast it creates with the traditional Victorian Pavilion stand opposite.

A short way up the road,

we pass St John's Wood Underground station, where palm trees add a uniquely exotic flavour to this already elegant neighbourhood. Then we emerge in the Swiss Cottage one-way system, where there really is a pub called Ye Olde Swiss Cottage. The original is thought to have been built here around 1800, though the present building is a 2007 version.

The brutalist redbrick Odeon Imax cinema towers over it next door, though the venue is at least flourishing, and has just been updated to Luxe standard, gaining leather seating and more space.

The 13 now heads up the broad and distinctive Finchley Road, an urban dual carriageway that forms part of the foremost northbound route out of central London. It winds between tall, mainly redbrick Victorian terraces, undulating but gradually rising to the summit at Fortune Green, where Hendon Way branches off left towards the A1 and M1.

We continue directly north on Finchley Road, following a slow descent through Childs Hill to Golders Green, where a railway and bus station form the centrepiece of a busy traffic hub. These days the 13 bypasses the bus stands on its way farther north.

Not far from here, Finchley Road crosses the North Circular at a major junction known as Henlys Corner (after a garage that closed after 55 years in 1989). Over on the north-west side, look out for a bronze statue known locally as the naked lady. Actually called *La Déliverance*, it was designed in 1914 by French sculptor Émile Oscar Guillaume, and was a gift to the public from *Daily Mail* founder Lord Rothermere in 1927. Other copies exist around Europe, but some were suppressed, perhaps through unease about their content.

Following Regents Park Road, we pass through the busy retail and commercial area of Finchley Central, where the junction with Hendon Way can often

LEFT: **War memorial with the statue of St George slaying the dragon.**

LEFT: **Like an errant spacecraft? The Media Centre at Lord's cricket ground.**

LEFT: **Ye Olde Swiss Cottage, this version built just 11 years ago.**

LEFT: **The Odeon Imax at Swiss Cottage.**

**ABOVE: MV38222 emerging from the indoor bus station at North Finchley used at the start of southbound journeys on the 13.**

**BELOW LEFT: Golders Green war memorial.**

**BELOW RIGHT:** *La Déliverance*, **known locally as the naked lady, at Henlys Corner.**

cause tiresome congestion. We continue up Ballards Lane, where the suburban landscape is broken by the enticing entrance to Victoria Park (not to be confused with the one in the East End). Soon we arrive at a further commercial centre, North Finchley, where the 13 terminates.

A famous cinema, the 2,000-seat art deco Gaumont North Finchley, stood here for 50 years, but was demolished in 1987 and was later replaced by the sprawling ArtsDepot arts complex, surmounted by a tall residential tower. Under this you will also find a modern but rather forbidding indoor bus station, which is used by the 13 at the start of its return journey to central London.

The northern tip of this wedge-shaped island site is known as Tally Ho Corner – probably after a stagecoach halt once situated here, and a tavern of the same name. The current pub, though only built in 1927, has an appropriate period feel and makes a pleasant end to the journey. ● **PR**

**TOP LEFT:** Pigeons and French-style advertising at Tally Ho Corner.

**TOP RIGHT:** The Tally Ho pub has a pleasant period feel at the end of a long journey by route 13.

**BELOW:** The entrance to Victoria Park in Finchley.

# Croydon

*Today's services are provided by a subsidiary of the German state railway, but the two-letter code on its buses reveals the identity of the original operator of this 102-year-old facility that was rebuilt and extended following devastating wartime damage*

**RIGHT: Aerial view of Croydon garage, sandwiched between Brighton Road towards the bottom of the picture and the London-Brighton railway towards the top.** GOOGLE

**B**uses operated from Croydon garage display the code TC. The C stands for Croydon and the T for Thomas Tilling, which by the early years of the 20th century operated a significant number of buses largely in south-east London.

An agreement with the much larger London General Omnibus Company saw General provide three garages for use by Tilling at Bromley, Catford and Croydon. The Croydon facility opened on 23 January 1916. Tilling's London bus operations passed to the newly formed London Transport in October 1933.

Although officially this is Croydon garage, it has usually been described on bus destination blinds as South Croydon Garage.

This was the last London garage to operate open-top buses in normal service, having received five Park Royal-bodied AEC Regents built for C. H. Pickup of Dulwich as late as 1932. London Transport included them in its STL-class and they were allocated to Croydon in January 1934 for route 254 (West Croydon-Selsdon), which passed under a low bridge in Croham Road.

This arrangement did not find favour with the Metropolitan Police and the route was diverted in May 1934, allowing Tilling ST-type Regents with roofs to be used. In October of that year the 254 was renumbered 64. The STLs revived new, covered-top bodies built at London Transport's Chiswick Works.

During World War 2, Croydon garage was the victim of one the worst bombing raids of the Blitz, in terms of vehicle losses, when on the night of 10/11 May 1941 it was attacked first by incendiary bombs followed by high explosives. Fifty-eight buses were lost and many others damaged. There were also four deaths.

The fabric of the garage was almost completely destroyed and, following a clear up operation, buses were parked in the open for several years. The garage was rebuilt and enlarged between 1952 and 1954.

In July 1947 it was the second garage, after Leyton, to receive new postwar RT-type AEC Regent IIIs, beginning an association with the class that lasted until 1974. Croydon also operated London's first driver-only double-deck route in November 1969 when the 233 (West Croydon-Roundshaw) was converted from single-deck operation. The unique rear-engined Routemaster, FRM1, was a regular sight on this service alongside the XA-class Leyland Atlanteans, most of which were allocated to Croydon between 1969 and 1973.

During the mid-1970s London Transport suffered from a severe vehicle shortage, which led to it hiring buses from Southend Transport. Between September 1975 and February 1976, Croydon operated some of Southend's Massey-bodied Leyland Titan PD3s — with manual gearboxes long gone from London — on route 190 (Thornton Heath-Old Coulsdon).

When London Buses transferred its operations to smaller companies in 1989 in advance of privatisation, Croydon garage became part of South London Transport which was acquired by the Cowie Group in January 1995, making it the last of the big red bus companies to be sold. In late 1997 Cowie rebranded itself as Arriva with the South London operation becoming Arriva London

South. In April 2010 Arriva was acquired by German state railway Deutsche Bahn.

In 1990, London & Country — one of the privatised parts of what until 1969 was London Transport's Country Area — opened a garage at Beddington Farm, Croydon, operation of which transferred to Arriva London South in 1999. Following the loss of tendered service contracts, that garage closed at the end of March 2012.

Today Croydon garage has a peak vehicle requirement of just over 110 and operates nine daytime routes, one of which runs 24hr a day. It should be noted that the allocation of double-deckers can be a bit fluid.

## Schoolday services

Besides those nine routes, Croydon provides a single morning and two afternoon schoolday journeys on route 405 between Croydon and Purley. Go-Ahead London's Metrobus fleet provides the main service on this route. It also operates schoolday services 612 (Selsdon-Wallington County Grammar School), 627 (Worcester Park-Wallington High School for Girls) and 685 (Selsdon-Warlingham School).

The present day route 60, initially linking Brixton and South Croydon, was introduced as part of sweeping changes to the London bus network in September 1982. These changes came after the Law Lords ruled that the Greater London Council's fare reductions implemented the previous year were unlawful. Fares had then been doubled in March 1982, leading to a dramatic fall in passenger numbers.

The new route 60 replaced the 130 between Croydon and Streatham Common and route 118 linking Streatham Vale

**ABOVE: The part of the garage most likely to be seen by the public is the vehicle entrance fronting Brighton Road. The double-decker here is DW102, a VDL DB250 with Wright Pulsar Gemini body, a type that Arriva bought for its south London garages.**

## Routes operated by Arriva, Croydon garage

| Route | Vehicle type | Peak vehicle requirement | Contract start date |
|---|---|---|---|
| 60 (Old Coulsdon-Streatham Common) | Wright Gemini 2DL | 15 | 31 Aug 2013 |
| 166 (Croydon-Epsom) | Alexander Dennis Enviro200 | 8 | 31 Aug 2013 |
| 194 (Croydon-Lower Sydenham) | Wright Gemini 2DL | 14 | 26 Aug 2017 |
| 197 (Croydon-Peckham) | Wright Gemini 2DL Alexander Dennis Enviro400 | 12 | 1 Sept 2012 |
| 264 (Croydon-Tooting) 24hr | Wright Gemini 2DL | 15 | 29 Aug 2015 |
| 312 (Norwood Junction-South Croydon) | Optare MetroCity EV | 7 | 5 Sept 2015 |
| 403 (West Croydon-Warlingham) | Wright Gemini 2DL Alexander Dennis Enviro400 | 7 | 29 Oct 2011 |
| 412 (Croydon-Purley) | Wright Gemini 2DL | 8 | 31 Aug 2013 |
| 466 (Caterham on the Hill-Addington) | Wright Gemini 2DL Alexander Dennis Enviro400 | 17 | 31 Aug 2013 |

and Streatham with Clapham Common. Initially operated by Routemasters from Croydon garage, it was reallocated to Thornton Heath when converted to driver-only operation in 1983.

It took on its present form in August 1998 and the contract to operate it was awarded to Capital Logistics, which operated buses around Heathrow Airport. It should have been operated by new low-floor double-deckers, but these were not delivered in time. For a short period, the route was subcontracted to Stagecoach Selkent with additional support from Blue Triangle. Selkent was unable to provide assistance after January 1999, so Blue Triangle operated an emergency schedule with support from other operators.

This arrangement continued until mid-March when Capital Logistics finally took over the service with its intended low-floor DAF DB250s with Plaxton President and Optare Spectra bodies. The Spectras were the only low-floor examples of the type to operate in London.

Capital Logistics gave up operation of the route from April 2000 and the contract was reassigned to Arriva London South, operating initially from Beddington Farm garage although part of the allocation was transferred to Croydon for about five months from that October.

Retendering saw operation pass to French-owned Connex in September 2001. Following sale of Connex's London bus operations to Travel West Midlands in 2004 the fleetname Travel London was adopted. Retendering saw the route pass to Arriva London South from September 2016 with buses operating from Croydon garage. A new contract comes into effect from 1 September 2018.

## Operated for 70 years

There has been a route 166 operating in the Croydon area since 1948 and although its form has changed over the years, it has operated from Croydon garage with the exception of the years from 1992 to 1997 when the route was contracted to Stagecoach Selkent.

In its initial form it linked Chipstead Valley with Thornton Heath, with an extension north to Streatham Common for a short period in the early 1950s. Conversion to driver-only operation in 1970 coincided with it being re-routed away from Thornton Heath to terminate at Beckenham Junction. It was curtailed at Shirley in 1990.

A return to Croydon garage in 1997 saw the 166 take on its current form with its route revised to run between West Croydon and Epsom, taking it well outside the Greater London area. Epsom Buses was already providing a link between Croydon and Epsom, numbered 498, and a coordinated timetable was introduced with all buses numbered 166.

Epsom Buses gave up commercial operation on the 166, and consequently the entire route was absorbed into the London Buses network from 28 July 2001. These days most buses on London bus routes run over the whole length of a route, but the 166 is unusual in that although three buses an hour link Croydon with Banstead on weekdays, only one of these continues to Epsom.

A new contract starts on 1 September 2018. Initially there were concerns that Transport

of the long closed airport site in 1996. A change to its north-eastern terminus saw it take on its current route in 2003.

## The shrunken 197

The garage also provided buses on another well-established Croydon area route, the 197 that linked Norwood Junction and Caterham for much of the postwar era. It was one of the first London routes to be tendered and operation passed to London Country in August 1986. At the same time it was curtailed to run between Norwood Junction and Croydon.

Three years later, London Buses' South London subsidiary won the contract and it returned to Croydon garage, which has run it ever since. It was extended to Peckham in 2005.

Route 264 began in 1987 and ran initially between Tooting Broadway and Croydon on weekdays, replacing that section of route 64. Weekday and Saturday buses were provided by Merton garage but Croydon ran it on Sundays, when it was extended to New Addington.

All operation passed to Thornton Heath garage in late-1988. In 1990, tendering saw operation contracted to South London and it was rerouted to South Croydon Garage, although Thornton Heath continued to provide buses. It was cut back again to terminate in Croydon in 1991 and operation transferred to Croydon garage between November 1997 and early 1999.

Although Sunday operation returned to Croydon in 2000/01, in September 2001 the entire allocation transferred to Beddington Farm until that site closed in 2012, whereupon it passed to Croydon.

The route was extended from Tooting Broadway to St George's Hospital, Tooting in 2003. This coincided with the introduction of a night service, initially numbered N264; this was subsumed within the daytime route in 2004.

Several London routes have been shortened in recent years to aid reliability. An example is the

**TOP LEFT: Two Croydon-based Arriva double-deckers in the town. Alexander Dennis Enviro400 T65 is on route 466, while the 412 behind is DW507, a Wright Gemini 2DL.**

**BOTTOM LEFT: EMC9, one of the battery electric Optare MetroCity EVs that Arriva operates on route 312.**

for London would curtail the route's operation outside Greater London, but following agreement by Surrey County Council to subsidise the section within the county, it will continue unaltered. The Alexander Dennis Enviro200 single-deckers will be replaced by slightly newer vehicles of the same type.

Route 466 was introduced in 1998 when the Croydon bus network was changed in advance of the opening of the Croydon Tramlink. Running initially between Caterham and Shirley, it replaced parts of route 400 between Caterham and Croydon as well as the Croydon-Shirley stretch of route 166. An extension took it into Addington Interchange in 2000.

It was operated initially by Arriva London South from Croydon garage, but contract changes in 2003 saw it pass to Metrobus. Five years later Arriva London South regained the route and it returned to Croydon. The

current contract was originally due to expire in August 2018 but has been extended for a further two years under the terms of TfL's Quality Incentive Contract.

London's first civilian airport was in Croydon and from its earliest days this was served by local buses and, despite ceasing to perform this role immediately after World War 2, buses continued to display Croydon Airport as a destination until the early 2000s.

Route 194 initially linked the airport with West Wickham, but was extended to Forest Hill in 1936. Although Croydon had provided a few buses on it at times over the years, it was operated largely by Elmers End garage until that site closed in 1986; it then transferred to Croydon. Retendering in 1992 saw Selkent take over until it returned to Arriva London South 2003.

The route had been diverted to run to West Croydon instead

12, which for many years linked Croydon with Harlesden, usually in two overlapping sections. In 1972 the section between Peckham and South Croydon became the 12A, operated by Elmers End garage until Croydon took over in 1986, by which time it had been extended to operate between Peckham and Old Lodge Lane.

The 12A was withdrawn in September 1990, replaced by the 312 between Peckham and Croydon and the 412 between Croydon and Old Lodge Lane. Thornton Heath operated both routes initially, but the 312 was reallocated to Croydon in 1994. The section between Norwood Junction and Peckham was withdrawn in 2005.

In late 2015, this truncated 312 was the first route in London to be converted entirely to battery electric bus operation, using new Optare MetroCity EV single-deckers supported by two charging points installed for them at Croydon garage. A Chinese-built Yutong electric single-decker, built to London specifications, was tried alongside the Optares from April 2018.

Croydon garage gained a schooldays only operation of route 412 in 1993 and two years later the route was extended to Norwood Junction. In 1997 that route transferred to Croydon garage in its entirety and the following year it was revised to run between West Croydon and Purley.

## Once they were green

As explained in the article starting on p74, London Transport's Country Area operated an extensive network of trunk routes linking suburban London with the surrounding counties. In the Croydon area, the East Surrey company — a predecessor of the Country Area — began operating a service between Croydon and Sevenoaks in 1921, initially numbered S3. This became the 403 in 1924.

In 1936 it was extended from Croydon to Wallington and along with routes 408 (Warlingham-

Guildford) and 470 (Warlingham-Dorking) in postwar years provided a frequent service of green Country Area RT double-deckers along the urban corridor between Wallington and Warlingham, almost all of which was within Greater London. For many years, express buses ran in the direction of the peak between Warlingham and Croydon.

Rationalisation in the early 1970s saw the 408 and 470 withdrawn east of Croydon and converted to driver-only operation, while the 403 was curtailed at Warlingham. A new route, initially numbered 403A, provided a service between West Croydon and Tonbridge.

The 403 was the last London Country route operated by RTs, with the last example appearing in September 1978. It became a driver-only service the following year and was extended west

from Wallington to Cheam in 1980. Given that it operated for almost all of its length in Greater London, it was no surprise that the route was absorbed within the London Buses network from August 1986, but with operation initially contracted to London Country there was little sign of outward change.

Retendering in 1991 saw operation pass to South London from Croydon garage. At the same time the route was shortened again to run between West Croydon and Warlingham. London & Country won it back again in November 1994 and operated it from Beddington Farm garage. Operation transferred to Croydon garage in 2011 with a new contract, but another contract change will transfer it away to Go-Ahead London Metrobus from October 2018. ● **ML**

# BUSES™ FESTIVAL

## CLASSIC AND MODERN BUS EVENT

## 19 AUGUST 2018

### BRITISH MOTOR MUSEUM, GAYDON, WARWICKSHIRE CV35 0BJ

**FEATURES INCLUDE:**

- Restored buses and coaches on display from a range of decades and fleets
- Quality traders selling bus related items
- Modern PSVs and industry suppliers
- Free bus rides around the British Motor Museum and local scenic routes

**Check out the official website for vehicle, trade and exhibit listings**

**STANDARD TICKET PRICE INCLUDES:**

**FREE** Access to British Motor Museum

**FREE** Parking

**FREE** Courtesy bus from Leamington Spa train station *Kindly provided by Stagecoach*

**ADVANCE TICKET PRICES**

**Adult VIP: £40** INCLUDES STANDARD TICKET ENTRY PLUS EXCLUSIVE SHOW GOODIES

SAVE ££s when booking in advance

**Adult £10** (Save £4*)

**Child £6** (5-16 yrs) (Save £3*)

**ON THE DAY PRICES:**
Adult: £14 • Concessions: £12
• Child (5-16 yrs): £9 • Children under 5: FREE
• Family (2 adults, 3 children): £39

**Opening times: 10am-4pm**

NEW FOR 2018 VIP TICKETS ONLY £40 EACH!

Children under 16 must be accompanied by an adult at all times. *Savings against British Motor Museum on-the-day ticket prices. Deadline for advance ticket orders 12 August 2018.

VIP TICKET INCLUDES STANDARD TICKET **PLUS** EXCLUSIVE guided vehicle tour - EXCLUSIVE diecast vehicle EXCLUSIVE DVD - Buses Yearbook - EXCLUSIVE event badge and loads more goodies.

308/18

**TO BUY TICKETS** **Call: 01780 480 404**

**Visit: www.busesfestival.com**

**To exhibit your vehicle or trade, contact Julie Lawson on 01780 755 131, email: julie.lawson@keypublishing.com**
or visit www.busesfestival.com for more info.

# Route 27

Chalk Farm 27

BELOW:
ADH45043, an
Alexander Dennis
Enviro400H,
passing the Old
Packhorse in
Chiswick High
Road.

BELOW RIGHT:
The British
Standards
Institution's
Chiswick Tower
overshadows
a passing New
Routemaster.

Route 27, like many, has changed significantly since it was launched more than 100 years ago, but in one respect it has remained the same. Then, as now, essentially it ran from west to east into central London, then turned north.

In the past, however, it was much longer, stretching from Hounslow in south-west London to Muswell Hill in the north. Bizarrely, in the 1930s it headed briefly south from Hounslow on a long dogleg through Twickenham and Richmond, eventually making its way north-east towards Kew Bridge, then turning properly east into Chiswick High Road.

In 1991 it was cut back radically. The new western terminus became Turnham Green, halfway along Chiswick High Road, and the northern stretch was cut back to Camden Town. Then four years later the route was extended a short way north to Chalk Farm, and in 2012 it was extended about half a mile west to Chiswick Business Park. This is not far from the Chiswick roundabout, where the elevated M4 crosses the junction of the North and South Circular Roads.

At around 9miles, the 27 remains a long route, and is run at a high frequency (every 7 to 10min), requiring around 25 vehicles. London United, now part of the French RATP group, has operated the route since 2005, when it took over from First CentreWest. Currently it uses six-year-old hybrid-drive Alexander Dennis Enviro400H double-deckers. Subjectively, they are smart, modern and well turned out.

The route joins the High Road from Chiswick Business Park, a modern estate of gleaming metallic office buildings, under the shadow of the tall and equally gleaming tower of the British Standards Institution, which straddles the Richmond branch of the District Line at Gunnersbury station.

Chiswick High Road stretches a mile-and-a-half from here to Hammersmith – a broad, tree-lined thoroughfare flanked for most of the way by a mix of upmarket and local shops. Strictly speaking the area is divided into separate communities – Chiswick Park, Turnham Green, Stamford Brook, Ravenscourt Park (each with its own District line station), but if you're not looking carefully they can seem to merge together.

Look out for two pubs on the south side. The George IV at Turnham Green is a noted live comedy venue and the Packhorse & Talbot (only yards away) became the focus of a *cause célèbre* in 2014 when owner Greene King suddenly threatened to demolish it. The council intervened and ultimately created a conservation area around it. By the way, don't confuse it with the Old Packhorse, half a mile to the west on the north side of the street.

Also at Turnham Green is The Old Cinema, opened as a theatre in 1888, but operating as the Cinema Royal from 1912 to 1933. It has been converted into

a store selling what the owners claim is a unique mix of antique, vintage and retro goods, and over the years has been included in *Retail Week's* 100 best shops.

A little farther on is Stamford Brook bus garage, which was originally a tram depot, and is now the operating base for buses on route 27.

The High Road finally merges into King Street, Hammersmith's narrow main shopping street. This is one-way westbound, so eastbound buses on the 27 follow a northerly diversion before entering the thronging Broadway. Here they go up a ramp into the elevated bus station, which is enclosed by the modern office and shopping complex that takes up most of the Hammersmith one-way system.

Resuming the journey eastward on Hammersmith Road, we pass the redbrick and terracotta St Paul's Hotel – the remnant of St Paul's School, built in 1884 and reputedly the biggest school in the country in its day. Then we come to the austere *moderne*-style 1929 art deco frontage of the Olympia exhibition and conference centre, and round the corner the two giant arched halls that host bigger events such as the Ideal Home exhibition. The larger original hall dates from 1885 and is now Grade II listed.

Crossing the inner ring road near Holland Park, with its partial night-time barriers discouraging traffic from disturbing the favoured residents of Warwick Gardens, we reach

**TOP LEFT: The Old Cinema in Turnham Green.**

**TOP RIGHT: ADH45037 passes the exit road from Stamford Brook garage, base for the buses on route 27.**

**BELOW: The Lyric Theatre in Hammersmith.**

**RIGHT: St Paul's
Hotel, part of
the former St
Paul's School, in
Hammersmith.**

**BELOW: Art deco
style at Olympia.**

Kensington High Street where another art deco edifice, the former Barkers department store, towers over the area. These days it houses a selection of smaller shops.

Now the 27 turns north up Kensington Church Street towards Notting Hill Gate, passing the flag- and flower-bedecked Churchill Arms pub along the way. Crossing Bayswater Road, we find a short stretch of tourist-oriented shops on Pembridge Road – a hint of the busy street market farther down Portobello Road, which dives off to our left. Pembridge Road itself is a quiet oasis of upmarket white Georgian villas, curving slowly round to the east until we merge into the more bustling Westbourne Grove.

On the day I travelled the route, a 'Spring Contemporary' art exhibition was under way here at Maddox Gallery, a recently opened branch of an international gallery chain. The front window display appeared to consist of substantial live trees with pink and white blossom bursting out through the glazing

and into the street.

On Bishops Bridge Road we pass close to Whiteleys of Queensway, another one-time department store that is now a shopping and leisure centre. We swing right towards Paddington station, then left into Praed Street, passing the works for the forthcoming cross-London Elizabeth Line.

Leaving behind the shops and snack bars, thronging with travellers and lunchtime workers, we thread our way through slow traffic across Edgware Road and on to the Marylebone Road dual carriageway: a painstaking process that can add long delays to the service at peak times.

Here we join the torrent of traffic descending from the Westway flyover, passing the Royal Academy of Music, Baker Street station and Madame Tussauds waxworks. The green dome of the Planetarium is a striking landmark, though astronomical presentations ceased 12 years ago, and the building now serves simply as an extension to the Tussauds complex.

**ABOVE LEFT: The barriers that lower at night to protect the peace of Warwick Gardens.**

**MIDDLE LEFT: A dental specialist in a mews off Kensington Church Street.**

**BELOW: Blossoming live trees burst from the windows of the Maddox Gallery in Westbourne Grove.**

Finally, not far beyond Regent's Park, we turn north on Hampstead Road, passing the giant white art deco Carreras building and Leslie Green's oxblood-tiled Mornington Crescent Underground station, built in 1907. Then we fork left past the domed white Koko music venue, opened in 1900 as the Camden Theatre and now Grade II listed, and head up the broad one-way Camden High Street. On the return journey, buses have to go the long way round via Kentish Town Road.

The stretch passing Camden Lock is bursting with tourists, and the activity doesn't stop here. Just beyond Regents Canal and the railway bridge we come to Stables Market, originally used by Pickfords to house canal barge horses. Overall, the markets in Camden are said to represent the fourth-biggest tourist draw in London, attracting a quarter of a million visitors a week.

Journey's end is a short way beyond Stables Market in Chalk Farm Road – really just an extension of Camden's town centre. A few paces farther on is the Roundhouse, a celebrated concert venue since 1964, but built in 1847 as a railway engine shed. And a little farther up the hill is another tube station by Leslie Green. Both this and Mornington Crescent are Grade II listed, and this one has Green's longest frontage. ● **PR**

**ABOVE: Rear view of ADH45042 passing Madame Tussauds.**

**BELOW: The Planetarium dome at Madame Tussauds.**

**TOP LEFT: Royal Academy of Music.**

**TOP RIGHT: Crowds throng Camden Market.**

**MIDDLE: The Roundhouse, originally an engine shed for steam railway locomotives.**

**BOTTOM: The Grade II-listed Chalk Farm Underground station, with the longest frontage designed by Leslie Green and opened in 1906/07.**

# They kept on coming

*The heart of shopping in the West End has been served for decades by a seemingly endless stream of red double-deckers, but if all goes to plan they will soon be taken away to open Oxford Street purely to pedestrians*

Y ou're standing on a pavement thronging with shoppers, and Routemasters (the original kind) are coming at you in an apparently endless stream. After a while, it seems there can scarcely be this many Routemasters in the whole world. They just keep coming.

This was London's Oxford Street in the late 1960s...and the late 1970s, and 1980s, and 1990s. By then it seemed that Routemasters would last forever, and would always represent the defining look of Oxford Street, in transport terms at least.

Oxford Street runs west to east through London's West End, stretching 1.2miles (1.9km) between the Edgware Road/Park Lane junction in the west and the Tottenham Court Road/Charing Cross Road junction in the east.

It has famous landmarks at both ends – to the west, John Nash's Marble Arch, which dates from 1827, and to the east, property tycoon Harry Hyams's 33-storey Centre Point, dating from 1966. Roughly halfway along is Oxford Circus, where Oxford Street is crossed by the north-south Regent Street.

Oxford Street itself dates back to the 18th century, when

**ABOVE: Centre Point, where the eastern end of Oxford Street meets Tottenham Court Road, undergoing refurbishment in 2014, is dwarfing a New Routemaster in the street below. Work to accommodate the Elizabeth Line has taken up much of the pavement around Tottenham Court Road Underground station.**

part of its hinterland was owned by the Earl of Oxford. However, it was in the 19th century that it became recognised as an entertainment and shopping venue. Nowadays it is reported to be home to 300 retail stores, including big names such as Selfridges, Debenhams, House of Fraser, John Lewis and Marks & Spencer, and to be visited by more than 100million people a year.

The Routemasters that plied the street for so many years were more than just a backdrop; they were also highly practical. As shopping streets go, Oxford Street is long. Suppose you wanted to speed your progress from the M&S store near the western end to John Lewis, halfway along; you could hop on almost any bus.

They might not all serve every bus stop, but with frequent traffic lights and the slow pace of traffic, it was easy enough to board one almost anywhere. The same applied with the RT and STL types and others that came before them.

### Ever-changing Routemasters

Over the years the Routemasters gradually changed in appearance. Originally a largely uniform red, they gained new fleetnames during the 1980s, when London's buses were divided into area-wide operating units – South London and London United, for instance. Then, as those units were privatised, new livery variants were introduced: still red, but with distinctive company logos and splashes of additional colour.

Perhaps the Routemasters' high point was in the early 1990s. In their twilight years they had come in for an unexpected refurbishment campaign, and their new private-sector owners were rather proud of them. Liveries like Stagecoach's respectful red with gold-leaf fleetname positively gleamed.

Looking back, the torrent of Routemasters that defined Oxford Street for so long gave a slightly deceptive picture

**LEFT: Feeding pigeons by Marble Arch as an eastbound New Routemaster slips past.**

**BELOW: Refurbished Routemasters pass outside Debenhams in April 2004. Heading towards the Aldwych on route 13 is RM331, refurbished with a new engine and gearbox for Transport for London and allocated to London Sovereign. A badge on the back of RM2109 on route 12 advertises that this Go-Ahead vehicle has a Scania engine.** MARK LYONS

      **The London Bus**

**ABOVE: Metroline livery — essentially the addition of a discreet blue skirt and radiator grille — applied to Routemaster RML2728, making its way west along Oxford Street on route 390, which was created when route 10 was split into two overlapping services.**

**RIGHT: For a few months in 1979, bright red and yellow Routemasters provided the Shop Linker service connecting Oxford Street and other West End retail attractions with Knightsbridge.**

of transport in the capital. By the late 1990s, when around a dozen Routemaster routes still converged on the street, by far the majority of bus routes elsewhere in London were run by much more modern buses. But open-platform Routemasters were kept on these high-profile routes precisely because of their accessibility and speed of boarding.

It couldn't go on forever. They finally disappeared from London's premier shopping street between 2003 and 2005, replaced for the most part by rear-engined double-deckers, but also in some cases by articulated bendybuses or other single-deckers.

Those modern buses continued to parade along Oxford Street in prodigious numbers for the next 12 years. Bendybuses disappeared in 2011, but double- and single-deckers thrived. You couldn't hop on and off, of course, but at least you could board or alight somewhere on the street.

New Routemasters did briefly revive the hop-on/hop-off concept

in 2013. Two routes serving Oxford Street gained buses with this capability – the 10 and the 390. But the hop-on facility was withdrawn in 2016, so although New Routemasters continue to serve Oxford Street to this day, the doors stay closed between stops, and you can only board or alight at bus stops, as with all the other modern buses.

## Radical plans

All this began to change in 2017, after the Mayor of London, Sadiq Khan, announced radical plans that could alter the character of Oxford Street forever.

The aim is to remove buses completely from most of the street, starting with the western half – partly to reduce pollution,

In the next, more dramatic phase set to unfold during 2018, the remaining nine bus routes will be removed from the western half of the street. There are also longer-term plans to pedestrianise the eastern section, removing yet more buses from it.

## East-west, north-south

It should be remembered that in the tide of buses flowing along Oxford Street, by no means all have been running on east-west routes, despite appearances. Historically, many arrived from the north or south, and simply turned on to Oxford Street to run part-way or all the way along it, then turned off again to continue their journey.

Remember, too, that in the past London bus routes were much longer than they are now, and far more of them were cross-town routes. Over the years, many have been cut back to improve reliability. This means that for more and more bus routes, Oxford Street became a starting point or destination, rather than part of a longer journey.

An intriguing example is route 88. Back in the 1980s, when it was operated by Routemasters, it started at Acton in west London, ran directly eastwards along Oxford Street as far as Oxford Circus, then turned south down Regent Street and headed onwards to Clapham in south London.

In 1990 the western section

**LEFT: June 1989 at Oxford Circus and Routemasters again seem to be everywhere. London Buses had just been restructured into smaller operating companies, so RML2326 on route 6 was allocated to London Forest while CentreWest was running RML2467 on the 15.**

**BELOW: A reminder in December 2017 of an Oxford Street era that came and went within the lifetime of the Routemaster. Red Arrow single-deckers linked Victoria and Oxford Circus from April 1966 until August 1988. Typical of the type of buses used in the 1960s and 1970s are the two preserved AEC Merlins taking part in this recreation of the service.**
RICHARD GODFREY

partly to allow the street to be pedestrianised. According to official thinking, both retailers and shoppers will benefit from the resultant traffic-free environment.

It will be a massive upheaval, and some see it as a withdrawal of the very lifeblood of the street: the means to deliver shoppers and retail workers to it. Reportedly, in recent times up to 220,000 people have been travelling by bus along part of the street every day, and many will now have to break their journey or start and finish it on foot.

Official thinking is that this is a small price to pay. Estimates vary, but it is thought that in recent years more than 300 buses an hour were using Oxford Street

at peak times. Some of the major retailers were complaining that congestion and pollution were driving away customers. The plan to remove the buses will provide a severe test of that argument.

Buses have not disappeared from Oxford Street altogether yet, but the initial wave of changes in 2017 removed buses on five routes from the western half of the street – the stretch between Oxford Circus and Orchard Street, which joins Oxford Street from the north between Selfridges and Marks & Spencer's flagship Marble Arch store. These were the 6, 13, 73, 137 and 189. The first four of these had been original Routemaster routes almost up to the type's final withdrawal in 2005.

**RIGHT:** The last Routemaster in all-day service, beautifully refurbished Arriva RM2217, leaving Marble Arch terminus at the western end of Oxford Street around midday on 9 December 2005, complete with police escort, as these iconic vehicles finally bowed out of mainstream service. It was 40 years old and others were up to six years older.

**BELOW:** Nine years earlier, RM2217 — photographed turning from Oxford Street into Regent Street at Oxford Circus — was a regular on route 159, painted in this red and cream livery.

Street, and again was operated by Routemasters – actually increasing their numbers on the street. However, two years later the residual Oxford Street section of the original 88 was finally lopped off, and the service was switched to rear-engined double-deckers. Their northern terminus was now Oxford Circus.

Ironically, in this case an additional northern section was tacked on to the route in 2009, taking it up to Camden Town. So from running east-west along Oxford Street, the 88 ended up running north-south across it.

Other long routes have simply been curtailed somewhere in the environs of Oxford Street. Typical is the 159 (famously the final Routemaster route in December 2005), which once ran from Thornton Heath in south London to West Hampstead in the north – traversing most of the western half of Oxford Street in the process. In 1992 the northern section was dropped, leaving the route to terminate at Marble Arch.

Some routes were removed completely from Oxford Street in previous culls – among them the 15, which arrived in central London from the East End, progressed up Regent Street to Oxford Circus, ran along Oxford Street to Marble Arch, then turned north up Edgware Road to Paddington.

As late as 2004, a year before

the end of normal Routemaster operation, the very last example of the type to be built, RML2760, could still be seen frequently on the route. The Oxford Street section of the 15 survived until 2010 with modern rear-engined buses, but then the route was cut back to Oxford Circus, and three years later it was cut back again to Trafalgar Square.

For routes that have continued to serve Oxford Street, you could almost argue that it has gradually become one long, dynamic bus terminus. Admittedly, not many routes have ever started or ended in Oxford Street itself; instead, buses have tended to turn in side streets such as John Princes Street, just round the corner from Oxford Circus, or at Marble Arch. Nevertheless, Oxford Street has remained the real target.

## Where will they go?

So what is happening to all the buses that have been using the western half of Oxford Street?

The first five routes have been either diverted to new destinations that avoid the need to use Oxford Street (the 13 to Victoria instead of the Aldwych, for instance), or truncated just short of the affected section of Oxford Street (for instance, the 73 in Cavendish Square, just to the north).

Nine further routes are due

was discontinued beyond Marble Arch, and was replaced by new service 94 to and from Acton. This service again ran along the western half of Oxford

LEFT: The bendybus era saw these Mercedes-Benz Citaros replace Routemasters on route 73 for a time. This one is passing the John Lewis store.

**RIGHT: Newer types of double-decker gradually ousted Routemasters from Oxford Street. The Arriva vehicle on route 176 is L66, one of 260 Leyland Olympians new to London Buses in 1986/87.**

**BELOW: A Chinese-built BYD electric double-decker in the Metroline fleet — one of five built for trials in London — leads a New Routemaster westwards along the eastern section of Oxford Street, as a cyclist passes on a food delivery and a taxi mounts the central reservation to make way for the buses.**
GAVIN BOOTH

to be dealt with similarly, with several simply stopping short of Oxford Street (the 7, 98 and 113, for example). By the end of 2018, it is planned that only two routes out of the previous 16 will still run east-west along the Oxford Street axis – the 139 and the 390. These will be diverted via Wigmore Street, several hundred metres north of Oxford Street, and Henrietta Place, which is slightly closer.

After the initial pedestrianisation programme, the eastern section of Oxford Street will still be open to traffic. This part of the street has never had quite the cachet of the western section, perhaps lacking any high-profile department stores. It does however feature various other famous retail names such as Top Shop and

Gap. It also contains Marks & Spencer's Grade II listed Pantheon store, whose striking art deco façade was designed by Robert Lutyens, son of the more famous Edwin. It was named after an 18th century entertainment venue called (you guessed it) the Pantheon.

For the time being this section of the street will continue to be used by several bus routes – notably the 25, 73 and 390. But pedestrianisation is due to follow during 2019, so the reprieve could be short-lived.

Curiously, the extreme western end of Oxford Street could remain permanently exempt from most of these measures. The short stretch between Orchard Street and Marble Arch forms part of a well established and extremely busy north-south through route,

linking the Baker Street/Finchley Road axis with Park Lane and Grosvenor Place. Short of banishing all traffic from this part of the West End, it is hard to see how planners could even consider closing this piece of road.

Admittedly, Orchard Street and Gloucester Place, forming two parallel sides of a one-way system, are both currently being converted back to two-way traffic, and part of Orchard Street will in future be limited to buses and taxis. But that means some bus routes will continue to join Oxford Street from here indefinitely (the 13 is one); so even when the dust has settled and pedestrianisation has taken full effect, it will still be possible to see buses in Oxford Street.

In a small part of it, anyway ● **PR**

**BELOW: Buses share Oxford Street with large numbers of pedestrians, as well as licensed taxis and other road users. This is Oxford Circus, where the pedestrian crossing has been redesigned to accommodate diagonal movements as well as those made at right angles.**

**RIGHT:** Heavy snow in March 2018 brings a line of double-deckers — mostly New Routemasters — to a standstill at Oxford Circus.

**BELOW:** The view from the top deck of an eastbound double-decker in Oxford Street, with taxis, one of many cyclists, pedestrians and a turning bus all helping dictate the (lack of) progress.

**LEFT: The future? Transport for London's vision of a pedestrianised Oxford Street, viewed westwards from Oxford Circus.**

# Looking good as new

*Specialist companies keep London buses up the latest standards by refurbishing their bodywork and reducing their exhaust emissions*

**ABOVE: Vehicles refurbished in 2018 for new contracts include Arriva London North DW295, a Wright Gemini 2DL new in 2011, operating route 221 at New Southgate.**
RICHARD GODFREY

Contracts to operate London's bus routes are awarded for between five and seven years, but the buses operated on them are usually kept for between 10 and 14 years, sometimes longer and to keep them up to date they will usually be refurbished at least once during their life in London.

Why not replace them all when the contracts end? Consider the sums of money involved and where it must come from.

Running London's bus network costs around £2.1billion per year with the vast majority of that money going to the operators of its 700 or so routes. Fares income is just under £1.5billion per year and this gap used to be met through an operating grant

— in effect a subsidy — from central government.

This has been steadily reducing in recent years and ended from the start of the 2018/19 financial year.

This means that London is now the only major western city that provides a bus service without any form of public subsidy. It has been estimated that the impact of the mayor's fares freeze and the Hoppa fare, which allows passengers to make unlimited bus journeys within an hour, could be up to £700million over the next four years.

In a typical year, between 15% and 20% of the bus network is subject to retendering. The default position for new contracts is that they will be based upon new vehicles, but alternative bids based upon existing vehicles

may also be made, provided they are refurbished in accordance with Transport for London's standards.

The mayor has committed operators to ensuring that all new double-deckers used on Transport for London services from 2018 are hybrids and all buses in the proposed ultra-low emission zone (ULEZ) will either be hybrid or zero emission.

A new London double-decker can cost up to £290,000, but a five-year-old one already in the fleet is worth about £75,000, so there are clear financial advantages in using older vehicles on routes that do not pass into the ULEZ.

London's buses are intensively used and over five years a bus could well carry over 1million passengers.

## Workshops have closed

Large bus operators — outside London as well as within — used to maintain large central workshops to overhaul and substantially rebuild their buses every few years. London Transport's works at Chiswick and Aldenham did this on an industrial scale.

Chiswick undertook the mechanical work, overhauling engines, gearboxes and other vital parts, while Aldenham did the bodywork. Both ran on a production line basis and the RT and Routemaster double-deckers of the 1940s, 1950s and 1960s were designed to be overhauled at these facilities.

Originally intended as a depot for a planned extension of the Northern Line that was abandoned in 1949, the Aldenham site took each bus apart and returned it virtually to new condition to such a degree that it was highly unlikely that it would leave the works with the same body, engine or gearbox that it entered with. As London's bus fleet became both smaller and less standardised during the 1980s, the maintenance of such a large facility became difficult to justify and it closed in 1986.

Most other operators have also closed their central overhaul facilities and specialist providers have emerged in their place. These include Thorntons in Ashington, Northumberland and Bus & Coach World in Blackburn, Lancashire. In addition Alexander Dennis, the UK's largest bus manufacturer, has workshops in Harlow, Essex and Anston, South Yorkshire where buses are refurbished for London.

Many operators lease their vehicles for the duration of a route contract. At the end of the contract, if they retain the route on the basis of using existing vehicles, the lease may be extended. If not the buses will return to the leasing company and, in most cases, they will be refurbished for further use.

Specialist dealers such as Purfleet-based Ensignbus usually take on the task of refurbishing and selling vehicles. Although the vast majority of such vehicles pass subsequently to operators outside London, usually after special London features like the second door are removed, others may find their way back to the UK capital.

## Hants & Dorset Trim

One of the largest bus refurbishment companies is Hants & Dorset Trim, based at Eastleigh, Hampshire. It was established in 1986 by Peter Drew, who had been works superintended at Hants &

**ABOVE: Wright-bodied double-deckers of Go-Ahead and Arriva undergoing refurbishment at Hants & Dorset Trim.**

**MIDDLE: Hants & Dorset Trim working on vehicles being kept in London and on others being sold for service elsewhere.**

**BELOW: New drivers' seats are part of the package.**

Dorset Engineering, a company formed to take over the state-owned Hants & Dorset bus company's central workshops in Southampton.

Although focusing initially on interior trim, it branched out into bodywork and was bought by the Go-Ahead Group in 2006, becoming part of its Go South Coast subsidiary. The same year it acquired a paint shop operated by FirstGroup in Eastleigh and subsequently expanded into additional premises on the same site, allowing the Southampton operation to close.

Today Hants & Dorset Trim has space to accommodate over 25 vehicles at a time and has a two-booth paintshop. Current throughput is between eight and 10 buses in an average week, with around 75% of its work being for Transport for London operators.

On arrival at Eastleigh, the company assesses the condition of the vehicle. All damaged panels, internal and external, will be replaced and where necessary these will be fabricated on site. A

common issue with service buses is that minor damage has been subject to *ad hoc* repairs by the operating garage, which while quick, cheap and perfectly safe, is not attractive.

The coatings on handrails can become badly chipped though day-to-day wear and tear. Although some operators use either paint or powder coatings on these, Transport for London insists upon nylon coating, which is more resilient.

Hants & Dorset Trim has recently completed the refurbishment of nearly 200 buses for Tower Transit. These were new to First London and the work carried out included replacing the lilac FirstGroup bell pushes. A new floor covering is applied along with a non-slip 'tile' to delineate the wheelchair bay.

Door draught excluders are another item that simply wears out and, again, these are replaced. Additionally, if not already fitted, LED lights

will be fitted to the saloon and destination display; they are cheaper to maintain and more reliable than fluorescent tubes and form part of Transport for London's requirement.

All seat cushions are removed and the seat frames either repainted or replaced as necessary. Any graffiti will be removed and etched windows replaced. As befits its name, Hants & Dorset Trim is something of a leader in seat repairs and its trim shop is able to process over 1,000 units a week. In addition to having precision cutting equipment for moquette fabric, it also has a foam press able to mould new seat cushions with accuracy. A crucial aspect of Transport for London's refurbishment standard is ensuring that seats meet the BS7175 Crib 7 fire retardant test.

Drivers are not overlooked either. Refurbished buses are fitted with new seats to the latest standards, which include

**LEFT: New foam cushions ready to go into seats.**

**BELOW: RM1933 was one of four Routemasters that Hants & Dorset Trim refurbished for the heritage service on route 15.**

light bulbs has returned and the staircase has been treated to traditional burgundy metal step-edgings.

The previous refurbishment work was found to have lacked treatment to component undersides, which led to corrosion setting in, so new fully treated panels have been fitted where necessary.

Externally, LED driving lights helped combine traditional aesthetics with modern performance. Following a repaint in traditional red with a cream relief band, fleetnumber, London Transport fleetname and other lettering have been carefully copied and measured from preserved vehicles at the London Bus Museum and reproduced to a high standard in vinyl.

Sadly, Transport for London suspended the programme for financial reasons after only four of the 10 buses were completed.

Hants & Dorset Trim has also recently completed the refurbishment of 11 Wright Eclipse Gemini 2-bodied Volvo B9TL double-deckers for the high profile X26 service linking Croydon and Heathrow Airport (see p110). A new contract awarded in April 2017 saw operation pass to Go-Ahead's Metrobus operation and, for the first time, double-deckers were

clearly calibrated adjustment mechanisms that allow drivers to set the seat to suit their own comfort requirements.

Once all of the bodywork repairs have been completed the bus is given a deep clean and masked up before being painting in London bus red with a white roof. After this, new vinyl logos and lettering are applied and a final exterior clean is carried out before the bus returns to London.

## Two noteworthy jobs

Although the vast majority of refurbishment work for London bus operators follows broadly the same pattern, Hants & Dorset Trim has undertaken two particularly noteworthy jobs in

more recent years.

In 2015 it was selected to undertake a major refurbishment programme of the Routemasters employed on heritage route 15, linking Trafalgar Square and Tower Hill. Although not intended to be a restoration, the opportunity was taken to try and recreate a traditional look for these iconic buses.

Around a dozen years ago, a superficial spruce up included new seat coverings and fitting fluorescent lights. That has all been swept away, replaced with an original look of burgundy sidewalls, grey window surrounds and seat backs, yellow ceilings and traditional Routemaster seat moquette. Even the shape of the tungsten

specified in the contract.

Although the route is popular, particularly with staff and passengers travelling to Heathrow, it only covers around 35% of its operating costs. This is largely because of its overall length (it is by some margin the longest daytime route in London), its limited stop nature and the application of the low flat fare of £1.50. It was therefore not possible to justify new buses, but something beyond the normal London bus was clearly required.

The vehicles selected were new in 2010 and previously used on East London Transit routes in Barking. The work included removal of the centre exit and providing a powered wheelchair ramp at the front door, fitting luggage racks on the offside lower deck and installing USB chargers at all seats.

### Under the bonnet
A newly refurbished bus looks as good as new, but further mechanical work is necessary

to bring it up to current standards. All refurbished buses must be fitted with engine bay fire suppression systems that meet the latest requirements. Additionally, some operators will take the opportunity to make other enhancements including fitting external coolant level indicators. These make the driver's life easier and reduce the risk of breakdowns.

One area where a five-year-old bus will falls short of a new one is the exhaust emission levels from

LEFT: Go-Ahead's WVL331 at Eastleigh, awaiting refurbishment.

its engine. Urban air quality is a hot topic, especially in London where low emission zones are being introduced.

In June 2017, Transport for London entered into an £86million framework agreement to upgrade 5,000 buses to the Euro6 emissions standards that have applied to all new buses delivered to London since late 2016.

Five suppliers have been selected, Amminex, Baumot Twintec, Eminox, HJS and Proventia. The upgrade entails fitting selective catalytic reduction systems to the exhaust system to ensure that harmful nitrogen oxides are removed. Diesel particulate filters are also included to remove harmful microscopic soot particles that can find their way deep into the lungs.

The work is being carried out at bus garages across London and is due to be completed by September 2020 when the entire fleet will be at least Euro6 compliant.

A refurbishment and mechanical upgrade of a London bus costs in the region of £20,000 to £25,000 depending on the amount of work required. This means that for around a third of the cost of a new bus it is possible to have a vehicle that looks new and meets the latest mechanical and emissions requirements.

There could well be many more of them, for as Transport for London's budgets come under greater pressure, we can expect to see more contracts being awarded on the basis of existing buses. ● **ML**

LEFT: Go-Ahead's WVL331 at Eastleigh, awaiting refurbishment.

**BELOW: Work proceeding on one of the X26 double-deckers, including removal of the centre door and installing luggage racking downstairs.**

**RIGHT: The windows on this Scania OmniCity have been masked up ready for repainting in the livery of the operator that has bought it for service outside London. The centre door has already been removed.**

**BELOW: Looking good as new, this six-year-old Alexander Dennis Enviro200 is one of several that RATP Group's Yellow Buses subsidiary in Bournemouth bought after they came out of London service with Tower Transit. They have been refurbished, converted to one-door layout and repainted in the new owner's colours.**

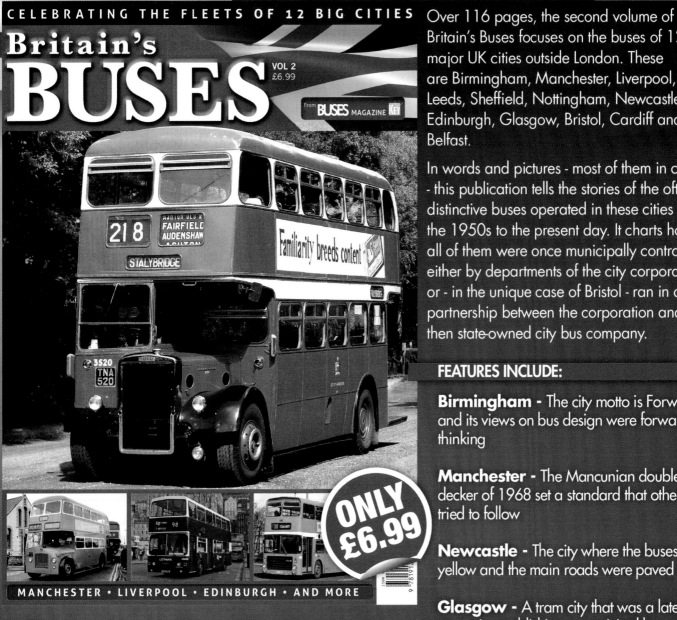

# Route 36

**T**he 36 is a relative
rarity these days
– a true cross-
London route
that penetrates
well into the suburbs in both
directions.

Many others have had one of
their ends lopped off in recent
years to improve timekeeping.
The 36 connects Queen's Park
in north-west London with New
Cross Gate in the south-east,
tracing a diagonal course across
the capital, and striking right
through the centre.

It dates back to 1911 and still
follows approximately the same
route as then, though it was
originally longer, extending
south-east to Lewisham and
beyond. Over the years it has
sometimes been supplemented by
two variants, the 36A and 36B,
which followed essentially the
same path but diverged at the
south-eastern end. These became
a permanent feature in the
1950s, but were dropped again in
the 1990s. However, the 36 itself
remains a high-intensity 24hr
service, with daytime departures
every 3 to 7min.

The 36 has been operated by
Go-Ahead's London Central
arm since privatisation in the
1990s. When I sampled the
route it featured an intriguing
array of different bus types,
mostly around six to 10 years
old. They included both diesel-
only and hybrid versions of two
makes – Volvo B9TLs and B5LHs
with Wright Eclipse Gemini 2
bodywork, and Alexander Dennis
Enviro400s. I also saw 12-year-
old Volvo B7TLs with earlier
Gemini bodies.

There was variety
in the liveries, too.
Some buses were in
London's current
allover red scheme,
but many were in Go-
Ahead's old London livery, with
grey and yellow skirt, and most
of these bore London General
rather than London Central
fleetnames. Both businesses have
long been part of the Go-Ahead
Group, and the branding reflects
the mixed origin of the buses and
the increasingly standardised
identity of Go-Ahead's London
operations.

Following a renewal of the
contract to operate the route,
Go-Ahead is introducing a
batch of hybrid Alexander
Dennis Enviro400 MMCs —
including the first in London
with ultra-capacitors instead of
batteries — to replace some of
the older buses on the service,
and I saw two of these already
in use in April (complete with
London Central fleetnames). The
company has also been using the
route to trial Optare's all-electric
MetroDecker, which has been
converted from its original 2014
diesel configuration.

Subjectively, in the age of
the hybrid bus I found I was

beginning to think of the diesel-only vehicles as sounding rather noisily 'industrial' both inside and out. Upstairs, I preferred the Enviro's rectangular front upper-deck window to the Gemini's, whose tall, arching shape had the odd effect of making the interior seem narrower than the Enviro's when I was sitting towards the back, though of course it wasn't.

At its northern end, the 36 starts in the centre of Queen's Park, a quiet suburb of smart Victorian terraced housing. It was once home to Queen's Park Rangers football club – which quit the area for Shepherd's Bush more than 100 years ago. Now the main feature is the park itself.

From here we thread our way through the quiet terraced streets of West Kilburn, passing the Victorian Chippenham pub and hotel, which has sometimes served as the 36's northern terminus. We turn briefly south-west on Elgin Avenue, then make a sharp turn east on to the Harrow Road.

Not far beyond Regent's Canal the road converges with the Westway flyover, which we pass under at Royal Oak. The rustic name of this district belies its character; its main feature seems to be the swathe of railway tracks heading west out of Paddington.

Crossing the railway on a modest girder bridge, we find ourselves among the elegant white terraced villas of Westbourne Park and Porchester Square. Writer Thomas Hardy lived in this area for a while, but reportedly was not happy here, and eventually returned to his native West Country to write his famous novels.

Now we turn east along Bishop's Bridge Road, then south towards Paddington station and central London. From here it's a short hop to Edgware Road, a busy thoroughfare featuring offices, multi-ethnic shops and blocks of flats. Then after half a mile we've arrived at the intensely busy one-way system of Marble Arch. Oxford Street stretches away to the east, but we turn right on to Park Lane on our way to Hyde Park Corner and Victoria.

**TOP:** An ornate gatehouse on a corner of Queen's Park close to the 36 terminus.

**MIDDLE:** Pollarded trees in Queen's Park.

**BOTTOM:** The apparently abandoned Chippenham Hotel in Shirland Road, West Kilburn.

Rounding the one-way system at Victoria among extravagantly elaborate modern office and retail developments, we bypass the bus station itself, continuing south-west along Vauxhall Bridge Road. It's a mile to the River Thames, and progress past the offices, flats and embassies and can be slow, especially at the approach to the junction with the multi-lane Grosvenor Road, just before Vauxhall Bridge. Even the bus lane cannot entirely mitigate the delays caused by the long red traffic light phases here.

**ABOVE: Volvo B9TL WVL292, still carrying traces of its original livery, heading east along Harrow Road.**

**RIGHT: WVL281 crossing Lord Hills Bridge at Royal Oak.**

Looming on the south bank of the river is the striking green and cream MI6 headquarters building, dramatically (and of course fictitiously) blown up in the Bond film *Skyfall*. Adjacent to it, the recently developed Vauxhall bus station has helped give a much brighter look to what was formerly a rather drab landscape. High-rise developments on both banks of the river underline the regeneration the area has seen.

As we move on past the Victorian apartment blocks of Kennington, a notable landmark is the Oval cricket ground, home to Surrey County Cricket Club. Look out for the disused circular gasometer frame towering over it; it has come to be regarded as iconic, and plans to demolish it in 2013 provoked a public outcry.

Our south-west trajectory now takes us across the busy A3 Brixton Road and on to Camberwell, a busy town whose village green has recently been restored and improved.

From here we turn directly east towards Peckham, another traditional south London township, and now ethnically very diverse. On the way, look out on the left for the Camberwell College of Arts.

You might spot a yellow Reliant three-wheeler van here on the forecourt of the Best Western Hotel. It bears the livery of Trotters Independent Trading, Del Boy's business

in the television comedy *Only Fools and Horses*, which was set in Peckham. However, this is a Reliant Robin van, whereas the vehicle used in the show was a Reliant Regal Supervan.

In Peckham itself, landmarks include the futuristic Peckham Library, partly funded by European Union regeneration investment, and the Peckham Peace Wall, where Post-It messages written after the riots

of 2011 have been captured in ceramic as a permanent appeal for reconciliation.

A station name displayed prominently on a railway bridge just east of Peckham town centre provides a reminder that the 36 runs between Queen's Park and Queens Road. Actually, though, the route continues a little farther east from here, passing through an elegant landscape of Victorian housing as we approach the bustling junction with New Cross Road and reach journey's end at New Cross Gate. ● **PR**

**TOP LEFT: Celbridge Mews, off Porchester Road.**

**TOP RIGHT: Elegant white terrace and lush garden in Porchester Square.**

**MIDDLE: The view of Paddington station from route 36.**

**BOTTOM: Enviro400 E249 in Grosvenor Place, on its approach to Victoria.**

RIGHT:
Contrasting architecture on Grosvenor Road, on the north bank of the River Thames.

TOP MIDDLE:
A northbound WVL406 crossing Vauxhall Bridge with the MI6 building behind.

BOTTOM LEFT:
Del Boy's Reliant van – except it isn't – on display in Peckham.

**ABOVE:** Part of the new Vauxhall skyline.

**LEFT:** The redundant gasometer viewed from the Oval cricket ground.

**BOTTOM MIDDLE & RIGHT:** The Peckham Peace Wall.

# Edgware **has the** edge

*Once served by electric trolleybuses and classic London Transport diesel double-deckers, this northern suburb is home to two red bus operators and is served by a colourful out-of-town operation*

**ABOVE: Edgware station forecourt in June 1986. Three London Buses M-class MCW Metrobuses are operating routes 221, 288 and 240, while a Routemaster prepares to leave on the 113 to Oxford Circus and a green London Country Leyland Olympian is on the 142.**

When the Romans headed north out of Londinium they extended Watling Street, which had already been established across Kent. Thirteen or so miles from the city centre they encountered Eggesweir, a fishing pool.

By the early 1200s, a farm had been established at Edgwarebury, 500 years later a turnpike trust was charging for the upkeep of this stretch of Watling Street and railways reached the community in 1867. The Underground was extended north from Golders Green in 1924.

Today's High Street, Edgware runs north/south along Watling Street between Stonegrove and Burnt Oak Broadway and from February to November 1903

a horse bus ran on Sundays between Cricklewood and Edgware, becoming a daily service from April to December 1904 when the Metropolitan Electric Tramways Company introduced a tram service (probably the 66) between Cricklewood and Edgware, extended in 1907 to Canons Park, known nowadays as Canons Corner.

The London General company ran its bus route 105 between Kilburn and Watford straight along the Edgware Road via Canons Park. During 1914 this was renumbered 142.

Tram routes were developed and altered and by July 1933, when London Transport took over, the 64 linked Edgware and Paddington, while the 66 linked Acton with Canons Park. But trams were about to give way

to trolleybuses and this change came to Edgware in July and August 1936 when trolleybuses 645 (Edgware-North Finchley), 664 (Edgware-Paddington Green) and 666 (Edgware-Hammersmith Broadway) were introduced. The 645 was extended from Edgware to Canons Park in June 1938 to serve new housing.

Trolleybuses on route 666 had to complete a U-turn manoeuvre across the dual carriageway in Edgware. Many occasions saw drivers attempt this turn with vigour, resulting in the booms atop the trolleybus becoming detached from the wires overhead. Thus the sight of the long bamboo pole from beneath the vehicle, brought into use to retrieve the errant booms and attach them back to the power source.

Similar occurred at the Canons

**ABOVE: N1-class AEC trolleybus 1623 on route 666 to Edgware.** J. H. ASTON/MALCOLM PAPES COLLECTION

**LEFT: AEC Swift SMS60, with Park Royal body, operating local route 288 in Broadfields in June 1971 when it was little more than a year old.**

Corner end of the route when vigorous circumnavigation of the roundabout created the same result. Simple pleasures kept us entertained for hours back then.

The trolleybus service ran largely unaltered until 3 January 1962 when Routemaster motorbuses took over on what became routes 245 (North Finchley-Stanmore Station) and 266 (Edgware Station-Hammersmith). The 245 and the 245A added later were replaced in September 1968 when route 251 was extended from Burnt Oak to Stanmore.

## Radical change

A more radical change in June 1970 cut the 266 back to Colindale, replaced by new route 32 between Edgware and Kilburn Park stations, still operated with Routemasters. The 142

was shortened then to operate between Watford and Colindale, its RT-class double-deckers replaced by SMS-class AEC Swift single-deckers.

Several other routes have operated along the High Street, such as the 107 to Queensbury (now withdrawn in favour of the cross-town 288), 204 to Wembley and Sudbury, 251 to Arnos Grove, 292 and 292A to Colindale one way and Watford the other, the 303 to Colindale and 305 to Kingsbury. Today, Station Road has probably the

greatest concentration of buses and routes as they either pass through Edgware or terminate at its bus station.

Along with the aforementioned routes, others to the west have over the years been the 18 extended through from Wembley, Paddington and London Bridge, 79 to Wembley and Alperton, 113 to Canons Park, 114 to Rayners Lane, 140 to Harrow and Heathrow and 209 to South Harrow. The 79 has remained fairly constant, while the 18 was shortened at Harrow in favour

of a new route 186. The 114, 140 and 209 gave way to a 286 to Harrow, which in turn became today's route 340.

In the opposite direction along Station Road, the 18 once had specially extended services to the bus overhaul works at Aldenham.

Another long route surviving from the 1930s is the 113, nowadays linking Edgware and Oxford Circus, the only one of the current daytime routes to penetrate the central Zone 1 area.

The 114 had once operated through to Mill Hill. From the 1930s, route 141 to Borehamwood became a 241 then back to a 141 before it was absorbed into an extension of the 107 from the direction of Ponders End, Enfield and Barnet. At one time this was believed to have been a contender for longest route on the network, nowadays cut back to New Barnet Station.

Route 288 is probably the most local service, introduced in June 1972 to serve the Broadfields housing estate, but later extended across to Queensbury via the High Street. Borehamwood had a second link added when route 292 began to serve the road, first from one direction then the other.

A route 104 operated from the 1920s and ran from the forecourt

of the Underground station through Mill Hill to Golders Green with General's B-type single-deckers. At one stage the 114 ran through from the west side to the Green Man at Mill Hill but was soon cut back to Edgware. The 104 was later severed at Mill Hill where the Golders Green section became route 240, while a new single-deck route 240A operated via different roads from Mill Hill Broadway to Mill Hill East.

Later changes during the 1960s saw the 240A replaced by an extension of the Routemaster-operated 221 from North Finchley. The 240 was eventually extended back to Edgware and operated with RTs then later by Routemasters.

Night buses first reached Edgware in April 1984 when the N94 (Liverpool Street-Cricklewood) was extended north. It was renumbered N16 in January 1991 and terminates at Victoria. It has been joined by the N5 from Victoria and the N113, a variant of daytime service 113, from Trafalgar Square. All serve different intermediate points.

For many years, Green Line routes 706, 707 and 708 passed through Edgware on their long cross-London journeys.

### Three garages

There has been a bus garage in Edgware since the first opened in April 1925. It was replaced by a larger one in 1939 and in 1984 by today's building, alongside the Underground line and opened in 1984.

This has capacity for around 200 vehicles and was created at the same time as the Broadwalk shopping centre and a new bus station. All three garages have been coded EW, which Metroline retains for the main part of the building.

RATP-owned London Sovereign operates from part of the building, using code letters BT, probably a legacy of when Borehamwood-based BTS operated here.

Postwar years saw London Transport operate prewar STL-type AEC Regents, their RT-class successors and for a short time the wider RTW-class Leylands. In the 1960s and into the 1970s RTs on the 18, 79A, 107, 113, 114 and 142 took passengers to Alperton, Enfield, Harrow, Kilburn, Oxford Circus and Watford.

My own favourites from my youth were the TD-class Leyland Tiger PS1 halfcab single-deckers bought in the early postwar period.

These transported me part of the way to and from school in Burnt Oak. I can still recall the sounds as they growled their way up Hale Lane out of the town towards Mill Hill East on route 240A. Those fine vehicles were eventually replaced by underfloor-engined RF-class AEC Regal IV, which although interesting were not as characterful as the Tigers. RFs remained in Edgware until 1977, when BL-class Bristol LHs took over route 251.

The Routemaster was the last crew-operated halfcab double-decker to frequent Edgware, lasting until route 113 was converted to driver-only operation on 25 October 1986.

### Competitive tendering

Edgware was one of the first parts of suburban London to experience competitive tendering for contracts to provide London Transport services.

The first in the area was route 142 (Watford-Brent Cross), which was awarded to London Country North West from 21 June 1986, operated from the former Country Area garage at Garston in Watford. To start with, existing Leyland Atlantean and Olympian double-deckers were used until new green and grey Olympians were delivered.

Next up was the 292 (Edgware-Borehamwood) on 6 June 1987 when it turned green with London Country North East,

LEFT: **London Transport replaced many RF-class AEC Regal IVs in the 1970s with Eastern Coach Works-bodied Bristol LHs like BL41, photographed in Edgware High Street in 1987.**

ABOVE: The multi-coloured phase of tendered London bus operations is typified in this view at Edgware station of Luton & District Leyland Olympian LR92 on route 340 being followed by a Northern Counties-bodied Olympian of Atlas Bus on the 107.

RIGHT: London Northern V30, an Alexander-bodied Volvo Ailsa new to West Midlands PTE, in Edgware on route 107.

although that did not last long. A failure to operate the service correctly saw it replaced on 22 February 1989 by a variety of orange buses both old and new with Borehamwood-based BTS. It in turn was later taken over by

Sovereign and the route turned blue and cream with brand new Volvo Olympians.

Route 79 (Edgware-Alperton) got buses of another bright colour from 21 November 1987 when the yellow ones of Southall-

based London Buslines took over. These were a mix of secondhand Leyland Fleetlines and then new Leyland Olympians.

The 107 (Edgware-New Barnet) was awarded to Pan Atlas based in Harlesden, which traded as

Atlas Bus, from 7 November 1989 using new white liveried Northern Counties-bodied Leyland Olympians from the start. It replaced London Buses' London Northern subsidiary, which ran ex-West Midlands Volvo Ailsa double-deckers — with front engines — on route 107 from Potters Bar garage.

Apart from route 142 which remained relatively constant throughout this period out of Garston garage, the other three routes chopped and changed back and forth between companies either by contract change or operator takeovers. After 30-plus years though, operation of the 142 returned inside the Greater London area in January 2018 when a new contract was awarded to RATP-owned London Sovereign's side of the Edgware garage in January.

London Buses' low cost Harrow Buses operation based at Harrow Weald Garage added variety with new MCW Metrobuses on route 340 from Harrow.

DT-class Dennis Darts with Carlyle bodies brought smaller vehicles to Edgware from November 1990 when Metroline introduced them on routes 251 and 288. Plaxton Pointer-bodied versions followed, later successive generations of low-floor Darts and their Alexander

Dennis Enviro200 successors.

January 1992 saw the introduction of new route 303 between Edgware and Colindale, followed a while later by a new 305 that was later re-routed from Colindale to Kingsbury. Both routes were introduced with new but smaller SR-class Mercedes-Benz midibuses with Optare StarRider bodies. Larger vehicles have since taken their place.

Route 186 linking Northwick Park and Brent Cross via Edgware was one of the first routes in London to be operated with low-floor buses, when Metroline introduced Wright Pathfinder-bodied bodied Dennis

Lances on 26 June 1994. By the end of 2005, every London route had low-floor buses, designed to be accessible by all.

Transport for London now insists on all its operators' buses being painted 100% red, so the colourful variety of the 1980s and 1990s has gone. However, Uno Buses — based at the University of Hertfordshire in Hatfield — runs its pink and lilac buses through Edgware on a regular basis on its routes 614 and 644 linking Hatfield and Queensbury. These run on London Service Permits granted by Transport for London to provide cross-boundary routes. ● **TW**

**ABOVE: Metroline TAL134, a Dennis Trident with Alexander ALX400 body based at Cricklewood garage, in Edgware High Street in February 2010.**

**BELOW: Uno 205, a Scania OmniDekka with East Lancs bodywork, operating route 614 on Station Road, Edgware.**

# SUBSCRIBE AND SAVE

## TO *YOUR* FAVOURITE MAGAZINE

London Bus Vol.5 - Special

**ROUTEMASTERS TO THE RESCUE**
VETERANS RUN DURING DOCKLANDS RAIL STRIKES

**BRISTOL RAPID TRANSIT**
METROBUS IS ON THE WAY

# BUSES

PROUDLY PUBLISHED SINCE 1949

**KEY**

Issue No.758
May 2018
Price £4.70

www.busesmag.com

## OPEN-TOP CHALLENGE
### LAUNCHES IN LONDON

**THAMES VALLEY REBORN**
READING BUSES REACHES SLOUGH

**NORFOLK ROUTES SAVED**
FOUR FIRMS REPLACE STAGECOACH

**£90M FOR AIR QUALITY**
FIRST ADDS UP GLASGOW COST

## BUSES Magazine

### The World's Biggest Selling Buses Magazine

As the World's Biggest-Selling magazine covering the bus and coach industry, *Buses* is renowned for providing comprehensive news, hard-hitting opinions and accurate information alongside entertaining and thought-provoking features. Illustrated with high-quality photography throughout and featuring the unique Fleet News section, *Buses* is the only choice for industry professionals and enthusiasts alike.

**www.busesmag.com**

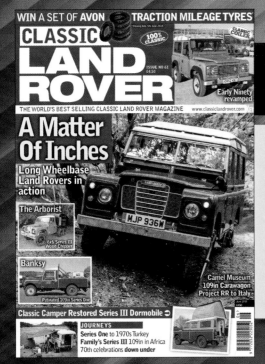

## Classic Land Rover
**Buying, driving, modifying and restoring authentic classic Land Rovers**

*Classic Land Rover* is the exciting monthly magazine dedicated to Series and the classic Land Rovers. Written by enthusiasts, it is the complete guide to buying, owning, running, driving, repairing, modifying and restoring pre-nineties Land Rovers and Range Rover classics. In fact, it is everything authentic series owners have been waiting for from their first completely devoted magazine.

**www.classiclandrover.com**

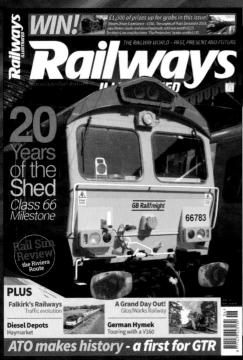

## Railways Illustrated
**The best coverage of today's railway scene**

Each issue of *Railways Illustrated* offers a comprehensive round-up of the latest news and topical events from the UK across the present day railway, including heritage traction in operation on the main lines. Supported by high quality photography and editorial from experienced railway enthusiasts, *Railways Illustrated* reflects the energy and vitality of the present day railway scene. *Railways Illustrated* also presents a regular photographic overseas feature, some semi-technical articles, and a popular practical series on digital photography.

**www.railwaysillustrated.com**

## FOR THE LATEST SUBSCRIPTION DEALS

**VISIT:**
www.keypublishing.com/shop

**PHONE:**
(UK) 01780 480404   (Overseas) +44 1780 480404

460/18

# Uxbridge

**Now part of Metroline, the 35-year-old garage in this Middlesex border town is partially hidden within an office block and operates a route network that has its origins in the 1920s**

Although Uxbridge garage has only been on its current site since 1983 there has been a bus garage in the town since 1922.

The original site, on the main A40 to the west of the town, was owned by the London General Omnibus Company, but Thames Valley Traction operated services on the General's behalf until 31 December 1928. These initially operated to West Wycombe (W21), Windsor (W22), Great Missenden (W23) and Watford (W24), although the Great Missenden service was soon cut back to Amersham and the Watford one was abandoned altogether. In 1924, the W21 became the 502, the W22 the 503 and W23 the 504.

When General took control of the operation, it operated route 503 from its garage in Langley. The 502 and 504 passed subsequently to Amersham & District, in which it had a substantial controlling interest, and the 504 was subsumed into the new Amersham-Oxford Circus express route that went on to form part of the Green Line coach network.

Langley garage passed to London General Country Services in March 1933, becoming part of London Transport's Country Bus & Coach Department in July that year. Routes in the 500 series were renumbered in 1934, the 502 becoming the 455 and the 503 the 458. A further route linking Uxbridge with Windsor via Iver Heath became the 457.

Today, First Berkshire continues to provide a link between Uxbridge and Slough via Iver as its route 3.

Under General control, Uxbridge garage provided buses for routes operating largely to the east of the town in what was to become Greater London. The garage is allocated the code UX.

Following creation of the Greater London Council in 1965, Uxbridge was one of only three London Transport Central Area garages outside the new authority's area (the others being Loughton and Potters Bar).

In early postwar years plans were developed to rebuild the garage although these were subsequently shelved and in 1954 an extension to the existing site was erected on an open parking area to the side of the

**Routes operated by Metroline, Uxbridge garage**

| Route | Vehicle type | Peak vehicle requirement | Contract start date |
|---|---|---|---|
| 114 (Ruislip-Mill Hill Broadway) 24hr | Volvo B5LH/Wright Gemini 3 | 18 | 3 Sept 2016 |
| 222 (Uxbridge-Hounslow) 24hr | Volvo B5LH/Wright Gemini 3 | 17 | 16 Sept 2017 |
| 331 (Ruislip-Uxbridge) | Alexander Dennis Enviro200 and Enviro200 MMC | 8 | 4 July 2015 |
| 607 (Uxbridge-White City) | Alexander Dennis Enviro400 and Volvo B9TL/Wright Eclipse Gemini 2 | 20 | 7 Apr 2012 |
| A10 (Heathrow Airport-Uxbridge) | Alexander Dennis Enviro200 | 5 | 29 Aug 2015 |
| U1 (West Drayton-Ruislip) | Alexander Dennis Enviro200 | 8 | 29 Apr 2017 |
| U2 (Brunel University-Uxbridge) | Alexander Dennis Enviro200 | 9 | 29 Apr 2017 |
| U3 (Heathrow Airport-Uxbridge) | Alexander Dennis Enviro200 Alexander Dennis Enviro400 | 11 | 29 Apr 2017 |
| U4 (Hayes-Uxbridge) | Alexander Dennis Enviro400 | 12 | 29 Apr 2017 |
| U10 (Heathfield Rise-Uxbridge) | Alexander Dennis Enviro200 | 2 | 2 May 2015 |

original building.

Work on a new garage finally started in 1979 in connection with the redevelopment of a site adjacent to Uxbridge Underground station and it came into use in December 1983. It is next to the bus station and sits under a multi-storey office block, so there is little of it to see from the outside. The administration facilities are on the first floor.

Following tendered service gains in 2017, an outstation — little more than an open yard with a couple of portable buildings — was opened in Wallingford Road on the Uxbridge Industrial Estate, although the main site still undertakes all maintenance work.

In September 1977, London Transport introduced two routes operated on behalf of the London Borough of Hillingdon. Numbered 128 and 128a, they were designed primarily to provide links between parts of the borough not well served by public transport and the Mount Vernon and Harefield hospitals.

The initial fleet of three ECW-bodied Bristol LH single-deckers, painted red and yellow, was replaced by Leyland Nationals in 1988. These services were incorporated into the mainstream London Buses network in 1992.

When London Buses introduced localised bus operators, Uxbridge was included within CentreWest operation, which was sold to its management team in September 1994 and acquired by FirstGroup in March 1997. CentreWest used local identities and these were identified as Uxbridge Buses.

During 2013 FirstGroup sold all of its London businesses. In April that year, the operations at Uxbridge were among five garages acquired by Singapore-based ComfortDelGro's Metroline subsidiary, which created a new company Metroline West company for the purpose.

Uxbridge garage operates 11 daytime routes under contract to Transport for London, two of them 24hr services.

## Routes 114 and 222

Metroline West took over operation of route 114 (Ruislip-Mill Hill Broadway) from London Sovereign on 3 September 2016. Five weeks later a night service was introduced on Fridays and Saturdays following the rollout of the night tube on the Jubilee Line.

LEFT: This is the open yard that serves as the Uxbridge garage outstation. Two Wright Gemini 3-bodied Volvo B5LHs are standing alongside a Volvo B7TL with TransBus President body.

It originally ran between South Harrow and Mill Hill via Stanmore but was cut back to Edgware before World War 2. Although extended at its western end to serve Rayners Lane in 1957, subsequent changes meant that it was running between Ruislip and Harrow Weald by the early 1970s. In the 1980s it was extended to Mill Hill East, via the route previously taken by route 140, which was cut back then to Harrow Weald.

Route tendering initially saw operation pass to Borehamwood Travel Services (BTS) in 1991 and this operation passed to Sovereign Bus & Coach in 1994. During July 2001, the low-floor DAF DB250 double-deckers previously used on route 60 (Old Coulsdon-Streatham Common) were transferred to the route. They remained there until replaced by new East Lancs-bodied Volvo B7TLs in 2004. Transdev acquired the operation in 2002 and renamed it London Sovereign. It was acquired by RATP in March 2014.

Although a route 222 linked Uxbridge and Hounslow from prewar days, operated by Uxbridge garage, that route was withdrawn in 1961.

It was replaced by an extension of route 223 which ran then between Ruislip and West Drayton. Ten years later, the 223 was diverted to run into

Heathrow Airport instead of Hounslow.

Its replacement was a reinstated route 222, once more run from Uxbridge garage. In 1994, it was one of five routes selected by London Buses to receive its first low-floor single-deckers. Fourteen Wright Pathfinder-bodied Dennis Lance SLFs were allocated to Uxbridge and operated the route until it passed

to London United in September 2000 upon retendering. A night service began in 2015.

Metroline West was awarded the contract to run the route from 16 September and operation reverted to Uxbridge, although vehicles are based at the outstation on Uxbridge Industrial Estate.

## Country connections

Country area routes 347 and 348 linked Uxbridge with Watford and Hemel Hempstead, but the level of service declined over the years and in 1994 Arriva the Shires withdrew the section between Northwood and Uxbridge. The remaining section, by then running only as far as Watford, was renumbered 8 in September 2000.

London Buses introduced route 331 to cover the Northwood-Uxbridge section together with parts of route U1 between Ruislip and Harefield. This links several communities with a fairly rural feel on the edge of Greater London and crosses the border four times.

It was initially operated by Arriva the Shires but passed to CentreWest on retendering in July 1996 and has been operated from Uxbridge garage ever since.

In 2015, Metroline West took delivery of 10.8m Alexander Dennis Enviro200 MMC single-deckers for route 487 (Willesden Junction-South Harrow). They turned out to be too long to negotiate one turn on the route, so after a period in storage, they were allocated to Uxbridge instead. Although they appear on any of its single-deck routes, they tend to make up most of the allocation on route 331.

In 1901 London United Tramways, introduced London's first electric trams on routes that included one between Shepherd's Bush and Acton over a stretch of line served by horse-drawn trams since 1876. An extension to Uxbridge followed three years later and in November 1936 trolleybus route 607 replaced tram route 7.

When diesel buses took over on 9 November 1960, the route was renumbered 207 and continued to operate from Hanwell depot. The following year Uxbridge garage began to provide a small proportion of the buses on the 207, initially only on Sundays.

In April 2005 the 207 was altered to run between Shepherd's Bush and Hayes End, with new route 427 covering the section between Acton and Uxbridge. Although Greenford garage provides most of the buses, Uxbridge provides a few to operate later evening services. This is largely for operational reasons, as Uxbridge also operated night route N207 between Uxbridge and Holborn.

The 607 number from the trolleybuses was resurrected in 1990 for a new Monday to Saturday limited stop variation of route 207. Operation was shared initially by Hanwell and Uxbridge but since 1991 has been provided solely by Uxbridge garage. Until 1995, specially branded Leyland National 2 and Leyland Lynx single-deckers were used, then new Northern Counties-bodied Volvo Olympian double-deckers in a modified livery.

On 29 November 2008 it was extended from Shepherd's Bush Green to White City bus station to coincide with the opening of the Westfield London shopping centre and a Sunday service was introduced on 11 April 2010.

Route A10 (Uxbridge-Heathrow Airport) was introduced in 1996 to provide a fast link to the new Stockley Park business park and Heathrow Airport. The initial contract was awarded to London Buslines, which First CentreWest purchased before the route started. Uxbridge has operated it from the start.

The first buses for the A10 were painted blue and yellow with route branding. Today's are allover red like most other London buses, but the A10 was one of 12 routes in the Hayes

**ABOVE LEFT:**
**First-liveried CentreWest TNL32923, a Dennis Trident with Plaxton President body, in Uxbridge on the 607 in 2010.**

**BELOW LEFT:**
**Metroline DEL2156, an Alexander Dennis Enviro200 MMC, in Heathrow Central Bus Station on route A10.**

area whose buses have been given some route branding as part of a drive by Transport for London to increase bus use. Five buses on the 607 have also been treated similarly.

## Minibus revolution

In the late 1980s, CentreWest was at the forefront of the minibus revolution in London and on 27 May services in the Uxbridge area were revised with a new network of routes branded as the U Line with U-prefixed route numbers and a fleet of Alexander-bodied Mercedes Benz minibuses.

Although some of these services have since passed to other operators on retendering, four still run from Uxbridge garage together with one other U-prefixed route introduced later.

Route U1 initially replaced the northern section of the 223 between Ruislip and Uxbridge, but was extended to Harefield Hospital and then Chorleywood. The northern section was replaced by a combination of Hertfordshire County Council tendered services and new route U10 (Uxbridge-Heathfield Rise) in 1994. It took on its current form in 2008. The U2 provided a circuitous link between Uxbridge and Hillingdon Hospital with an extension to Brunel University

introduced in 2009.

The U3 initially linked Uxbridge with West Drayton and was extended to Heathrow Airport in 1993, replacing route 223. Retendering in May 1998 saw operation pass to Capital Logistics, but it reverted to CentreWest three years later.

The U Line identity ended in May 1998 when a new contract replaced the minibuses with larger vehicles. The services remain operated primarily by single-deckers, some of which are branded for one specific route, but one double-decker is allocated to the U3 on weekdays.

Linking Uxbridge and Hayes, the U4 replaced the withdrawn

section of route 204 between Hillingdon Hospital and Hayes. It was converted to double-deck operation in 2004 and extended to the Prologis Business Park in 2012. Operation was transferred to Hayes garage between August 2016 and February 2017.

The opening of the Elizabeth Line from late 2018 will have a significant impact on services currently operated from Uxbridge garage. Three stations on the new line are on its bus routes and there is a large amount of new housing being built in the area. A new route, 278, is proposed to link Ruislip and Hillingdon with the Elizabeth Line at Hayes & Harlington. ● **ML**

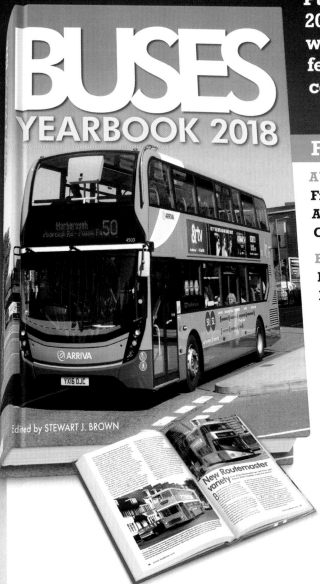

# A hard border

*There used to be dozens of bus services crossing the invisible boundary that separates Greater London from the surrounding counties. Most have disappeared over the past five decades although a handful remain*

**ABOVE: A notable cross-border red bus service surviving from London Transport days is the 81, today connecting Hounslow and Slough by way of the Bath Road to the immediate north of Heathrow Airport. RATP-owned London United provides it, using Alexander Dennis Enviro400H hybrid double-deckers like ADE42.**

The Mayor of London has a duty to develop and implement policies for the promotion and encouragement of safe, integrated, efficient and economic transport to, from and within Greater London.

The area in question is that of the Greater London Council, which existed from 1965 to 1986. It covered the whole County of London and most of Middlesex, plus parts of Essex, Kent and Surrey, a small part of Hertfordshire and the county boroughs of Croydon and East and West Ham. Its area was marginally smaller than that of

the Metropolitan Police district

The original intention was that it would have covered a larger area. A Royal Commission set up in 1957 intended that it would also include Sunbury-on-Thames, Staines and Potters Bar in Middlesex, Chigwell in Essex and Caterham, Weybridge, Epsom and Ewell in Surrey. London Transport, as it existed from 1933 to 1969, took in all that and more.

By far the largest of the bus companies that London Transport acquired at its formation, the London General Omnibus Company, had reached operating agreements by the 1920s with other companies in

the metropolis that fell short of outright ownership.

And by 1922, it had also made arrangements with three operators based outside London – East Surrey Traction, the National Omnibus & Transport Company and Thames Valley Traction – to govern the provision of bus services between London and its immediate hinterland. General took over the East Surrey company in 1929, renamed it London General Country Services three years later and acquired National's operations in Hertfordshire.

The first attempt to really define 'London' for the purposes of bus operations was the

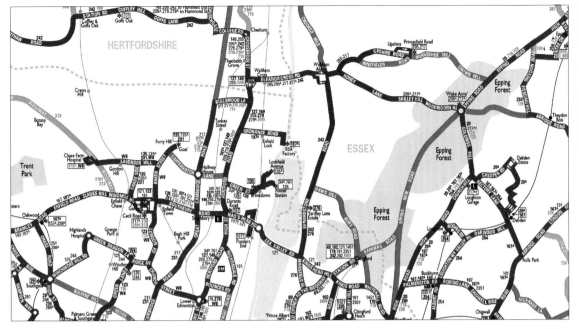

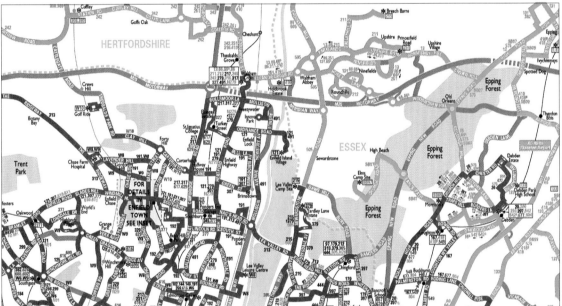

**LEFT & BELOW:**
**One graphic example of how cross-border services have changed between 1970 and 2018 is around Loughton, where there used to be a red bus garage. Forty-eight years ago, most services were provided by red London Transport buses running on roads shown in red, while the green roads were served exclusively by London Country. Today, Transport for London provides those on red roads, while Essex County Council and commercial operators provide those on roads now green.**
MIKE HARRIS
www.busmap.co.uk

London Traffic Act of 1924, which established the London & Home Counties Traffic Advisory Committee. Its area extended for about 25miles from Charing Cross and was bounded roughly by Harlow, Billericay, Gravesend, Sevenoaks, Reigate, Guildford, Slough, Amersham, Harpenden and Stevenage. This formed the basis of the 'special area' within which London Transport had virtually exclusive rights to provide bus services.

The special area protected General's acquisitions to the north and south of London, as well as the existing services of the other territorial companies. When London Transport was formed, some services were split at the border. For example, London Transport took over the Guildford-Dorking section of Aldershot & District's service 25, operating it as route 425.

### Red and green
London Transport's bus operations were split between its Central (red) and Country (green) Areas with the red Central buses running within the Metropolitan Police district. The Country Area took over services previously operated by London General Country Services along with those of smaller operators acquired during the 1930s. Its garages also were responsible for Green Line coaches, a network of limited stop services linking towns on opposite sides of London via the Central Area.

Many towns in outer London, such as Croydon, Bromley and Kingston, are obvious traffic objectives from the surrounding counties and an extensive network of Country services grew up linking them to the wider region. In 1970, for instance, it was possible to travel by Country bus from Croydon to Tonbridge, East Grinstead, Crawley, Horsham, Dorking or Guildford. Four Green Line coach services reached as afield as Windsor and Aylesbury.

Some red bus routes also operated well outside London. Some of these extended the reach of the Underground, such as the 81 linking Hounslow and Windsor, and the 84 between Golders Green and St Albans. General also was permitted to operate services outside the London area as it saw fit.

In 1970 the Greater London Council took control of London Transport, which had been in state ownership for the past 22 years. The notion of the GLC having political control of services outside its area was clearly contentious and the Country Area bus services were kept in state ownership, transferred to the newly created London Country Bus Services, a subsidiary of the National Bus Company.

Over 60 Central Area bus routes crossed then into what London Transport described as the 'out counties', while London Country operated almost as many bus services into Greater London in addition to 23 Green Line coach services.

This represented about 20% of London Country's mileage and one of its routes, the 493 (Orpington-Ramsden Estate), ran entirely within Greater London. Conversely, London Transport's 206 (Hampton Court-Claygate) operated entirely within Surrey while Sunday-only routes 205 (Upshire-Fleamstead End) and 205A (Hammond Street-Epping Forest) skirted the GLC's northern boundary. To the north-east of London, a sizeable network operated from Loughton garage, which sat outside the GLC area, all of which crossed the border.

## The Wood Green connection

Although London Transport or London Country provided most cross-border services, there were other operators. In 1927, A. H. Young, trading as The Empress Bus, launched a service between Southend and Wood Green. The following year the City Motor Omnibus Company bought a two-thirds share in it and although it initially retained the New Empress name, it painted vehicles in City's livery. The service was subsequently extended to Kentish Town.

In 1928, Westcliff on Sea Motor Services extended its Southend-Wickford service to Wood Green, where it opened a garage, although by 1934 City had acquired control of both routes. In a strange twist, Westcliff on Sea acquired its operations in 1952 with acquisition by Eastern National following in 1955.

By 1970 three routes were being operated — the 151 and 251 linked Wood Green and Southend while route 251 ran to Chelmsford. By then they were operated largely by 31ft long Bristol Lodekka FLFs dating from 1967/68. These were the double-deckers that featured in the popular television comedy series *On The Buses*.

The 351 was cut back to

Romford in April 1971 but continued to work through to Wood Green on Sundays until February 1973, while the 151 was withdrawn beyond Romford in 1976 and by 1981 was operating only between Basildon and Canvey.

In 1981 Wood Green garage closed and the 251 was converted to driver-only operation and revised to operate between Walthamstow and Southend. Falling passenger numbers saw withdrawal of the route, by then operated by First Thamesway, in May 2001. Eastern National also operated routes linking Romford with Basildon and Canvey Island.

On the opposite side of London, Thames Valley operated two services linking Reading with London, route A via Wokingham and Staines and B via Slough. These were renumbered 300 and 310 respectively in 1976 and, following deregulation of long distance services in 1980, were relaunched as Londonlink. That year also saw Reading Transport and Southend Transport launch a joint service linking the two towns via London. By 1982 the service was operated solely by Reading Transport, running only as far east as Aldgate, and it ceased in 2000.

Independent operators provided limited services including Golden Miller, which operated three services in the Feltham area. One of these crossed the GLC boundary to terminate in Shepperton.

### Fares and frequencies

The GLC set fares and frequencies within Greater London for London Transport and London Country services. This meant that London Country was effectively acting as a contractor to London Transport.

For as long as bus services were profitable (or at least covered their costs) local authority boundaries were of little real importance.

As the need for subsidies increased, councils started to look more closely at the cost of providing services and where they went. Local government can

be very parochial and councils' interests rarely extend beyond their boundaries.

The issue of cross-border services is probably most acute in Surrey, the boundary of which comes far closer to central London than that of most of the others. There is also the rather anomalous 'finger' of Greater London jutting into the county at Chessington and the borough of Spelthorne, which sits within the historic county of Middlesex but now forms part of Surrey, isolated from the rest of the county by the River Thames.

London Transport's costs were significantly higher than those of its green neighbour and from the mid-1970s an increasing proportion of London Transport routes was curtailed closer to the GLC boundary, with London Country providing some kind of a replacement service.

An early example was the withdrawal of the section of route 237 (then Hounslow-Chertsey) beyond Lower Sunbury in 1978. London Country's replacement service ran no farther into London than Feltham. More transfers followed in Banstead and in April 1982 the long established Central Area route 84 (Arnos Grove-St Albans) passed to London Country.

While London Country was the main beneficiary of such transfers, smaller operators also played a part. When London

Transport withdrew routes 201 (Kingston-Hampton Court) and 215 (Hampton Court-Esher) in 1980, Chessington-based Mole Valley Transport Service provided the replacement services, their frequency reduced significantly to just a few services running six days a week.

### Privatised London Country

In preparation for the privatisation of the National Bus Company, London Country was split into four operating units in September 1986, named initially London Country South West, North West, North East and South East.

Each was sold to a different buyer, but most of them have since come together again in Arriva ownership. The exception was the part of the North West company serving Slough, which passed through successive owners to become part of FirstGroup.

A critical change came in October 1986 when local bus services outside London — but not inside the Greater London area — were deregulated and opened up to potential competition.

This affected routes crossing the border. Several were not commercially viable and were not registered by their respective operators. The local authorities then offered for competitive

**ABOVE: Metroline operates the shortened former red bus route 242 from its Potters Bar garage on a commercial basis, with Alexander Dennis Enviro200s painted in this blue, white and red livery. The vast majority of Metroline's buses are all-red London ones.**

ABOVE: Once a green route, the 405 — shortened to run between Croydon and Redhill — is part of the red bus network, operated here by a Scania OmniCity in Go-Ahead London's Metrobus fleet.

tendering those non-commercial routes deemed to be socially necessary.

Many of them continued to be operated by former London Country companies, but tendering brought new names on to the roads. One of the more unusual decisions was Surrey's to award a contract to provide buses between Heathrow Airport and Walton on Thames to the West Midlands-based Thandi coach company.

Retrenchment by former London Country operators allowed others to enter the market with tendered and commercial services. This has been particularly pronounced in Surrey.

Today, Arriva only maintains a garage in Guildford and none of its operations crosses into London. As Arriva retreated, the gap was filled initially in large part by Tellings-Golden Miller (TGM) and Metrobus. TGM's local bus operations passed to National Express Group in 2005 and were acquired by Abellio — a division of the Dutch state railway — four years later.

Abellio withdrew from all of its Surrey County Council contracts in 2016. The subsequent re-tendering exercise saw the Rotala group's Hallmark Connections company establish a presence on cross-border bus work.

To the north, Uno — owned by the University of Hertfordshire — provides services linking north London with Hatfield, where its main campus is located. Although initially introduced to enable students to travel to the university from the outer limits of the Underground, services have steadily expanded over the years.

## Impact on London Buses

Deregulation also had an effect on London Buses' routes operating outside Greater London. Kingston (in Greater London but the administrative centre of Surrey County Council) and Staines had been linked by two bus routes operating on opposite sides of the River Thames since well before World War 2.

Deregulation saw route 216, running via Hampton and Sunbury, operated commercially by Westlink (a new low cost operating unit within London Buses) while the 218, running through Hersham and Shepperton, was operated by London Country South West under contract to Surrey County Council.

Although there were relatively few cases of competition, London Buses ran a service for three months between Kingston and Epsom that duplicated London Country South West's offering. Ten years later, Nostalgiabus introduced a similar service that also was destined not to last long.

London Buses also began to bid for tendered work, a process that saw route 84 return to red bus operation in 1986. It is now operated commercially by Metroline, one of the privatised former London Buses' companies, although it no longer reaches any farther into London than New Barnet station.

Metroline also operates route 242 (Potters Bar-Waltham Cross) commercially; the section from Waltham Cross into Essex and thence Greater London, at Chingford, was withdrawn in 1986.

In Essex, deregulation led to many routes in its area being contracted to smaller operators, such as West's Coaches. The impact of this, and the tendering of London Buses services on the outskirts of the capital, led to the closure of Loughton garage in May 1986.

## Transport for London

The creation of Transport for London (TfL) in 2000 led to three distinct categories of local bus service. Most are specified by TfL and form the London bus network. Their operation is contracted to private operators, with TfL specifying virtually every aspect of the service including routes, timetables and fares.

Initially, several routes not directly contracted by TfL were operated as part of the London bus network within London, charging TfL fares and accepting its tickets, under a London Local Service Agreement (LLSA). All other services required a London Service Permit.

Since then, TfL has contracted operation of as much of the London bus network as possible and there are now no routes operated under LLSAs. An

aspiration that no-one in Greater London is more than 400m from a bus stop means that the London bus network now covers more of Greater London than ever before.

The low level of bus fares in London means that non-TfL services struggle to attract passengers on stretches of road in Greater London that they share with TfL routes. The costs of meeting requirements of the low emission zone have also affected the viability of services that are, at best, commercially marginal.

Consequently, many long established routes have been curtailed short of the boundary. For example, route 310 used to link Hertford and Enfield but since October 2006 has not run south of Waltham Cross. The 348, which linked Watford and Uxbridge, has been cut back to Northwood, just inside Greater London, and has been numbered 8 since 2000. The section on to Uxbridge is now largely covered by TfL route 331.

Others have been withdrawn altogether, although in some cases TfL has stepped in and

invited tenders for the service, although many sections of route outside London have been curtailed. When route 405 (Croydon-Crawley) became part of the London bus network in 2001, the section south of Redhill was dropped. When the 216 was threatened with withdrawal in 2002, TfL brought it within the London bus network.

Some routes that have come within the TfL network have had their routes altered to reflect modern needs, for example route 370 now links Romford with the Lakeside shopping centre and no longer services Tilbury, while two TfL routes serve the Bluewater centre in Kent.

## The near death of Green Line

Perhaps the biggest change to cross-border services has affected the Green Line network, where increased traffic congestion and reduced passenger numbers mean that little is left of the routes that London Country inherited in 1970.

The Green Line brand is now owned by Arriva, which provides two services from Victoria to

Luton Airport (755 and 757) and one to Hemel Hempstead (758), while Reading Buses — owned by Reading Council — runs routes 702 (Victoria-Legoland-Bracknell/Windsor) and 703 (Heathrow Terminal 5-Bracknell). Arriva also continues to operate route 724, linking Heathrow and Harlow via Stansted Airport, although this is no longer branded as a Green Line service.

Transport for London's route X26 (Heathrow-Croydon) — described on p110 — provides a reminder of Green Line routes 725 and 726, which linked Windsor with Croydon and Gravesend, although now run entirely within Greater London.

One area that has seen a large increase in service provision is Heathrow Airport, which in 1970 was served only by London Transport local buses and Green Line coach 727 (Crawley-Luton), introduced in 1967.

Alder Valley, formed by merging Thames Valley and Aldershot & District, rerouted its Reading-London service via the airport in 1976, and in 1977 extended a service from Basingstoke into the airport. In 1983, London

**ABOVE: Although Arriva continues to operate route 724 linking Heathrow and Stansted airports with Harlow and many population centres and transport interchanges in between, it has ceased using the Green Line livery applied to this Mercedes-Benz Citaro that was new in 2006.**

Country introduced two routes linking Chertsey and the airport and Alder Valley extended its Reading-Windsor service there.

A major boost occurred from the late 1990s when the airport started to fund local bus routes as part of a drive to increase the proportion of people — passengers and employees — using public transport.

This brought a comprehensive network serving the Heathrow-Slough-Maidenhead corridor in addition to better links with High Wycombe, Staines and Windsor. This funding helped provide new vehicles, many initially in a silver-based livery with Heathrow branding.

Subsidies from the airport and local authorities have since been scaled back, reducing service levels. The commercial challenge of competing with TfL services means that none extends any farther into London, and from June 2018 Carousel Buses curtails its High Wycombe-Heathrow service to terminate at Uxbridge.

## Case by case

Local authorities stopped funding TfL routes in their areas by 2016. At the time, the Mayor of London said that although

TfL is aware of the importance of cross-boundary services, their future would have to be reviewed.

In 2017, TfL proposed curtailing route 465 (Kingston-Dorking) at Leatherhead. Following intense pressure from local residents, Surrey County Council agreed to provide £200,000 per year to support it. It has since agreed to provide a further £130,000 to ensure that routes 166 (Croydon-Epsom) and 216 (Kingston-Staines) retain their routes within the county.

Although cross-border buses benefit residents on the London side of the boundary as much as those on the other side, it is clear that TfL will look closely at the levels of service it provides. Nearly 20% of London's workforce lives outside the Greater London area and commuting is predicted to grow sharply as London's economy outstrips its housing supply.

However, while car ownership in London is relatively low and has fallen, the surrounding counties are among the most affluent areas of the UK and car ownership is high and growing. In 1971, 29% of Surrey households had no access to a car, but by 2011 this had dropped

to 13%, compared with 26% across England and 19% for the south-east. The average number of cars per household in the county was 1.5.

Although bus use in London has declined recently, it still stands at over 250 journeys per head per year. Across England as a whole the figure is 80 and in the surrounding counties it ranges from 21 in Buckinghamshire to 36 in Kent.

The Mayor of London's transport strategy sets out a vision to ensure that 80% of all trips in London are made on foot, by bicycle or public transport by 2041. It recognises that for London to be less car dependent, and to ensure that the wider city region remains economically successful, fully inclusive public transport must not only be provided within London, but between London and the wider south-east.

What is not clear is whether better cross-border bus services form part of a plan that spells out the need for better rail services and roads. Without concerted action by local government on both sides of the boundary, it is difficult to see how their decline can be arrested, let alone reversed. ● **ML**

# BUSES

## The World's Biggest Selling Buses Magazine

As the World's Biggest-Selling magazine covering the bus and coach industry, Buses is renowned for providing comprehensive news, hard-hitting opinions and accurate information alongside entertaining and thought-provoking features. Illustrated with high-quality photography throughout and featuring the unique Fleet News section, Buses is the only choice for industry professionals and enthusiasts alike.

### Featuring

**Fleet News**
Providing unmatched market intelligence of the vehicles registered to bus and coach fleets throughout the British Isles

**Global News**
The latest developments from the industry

**In London**
Route changes and operator news from the city

**National and international news**
The latest developments from the manufacturers

**Preservation Update**
Including rallies and running days

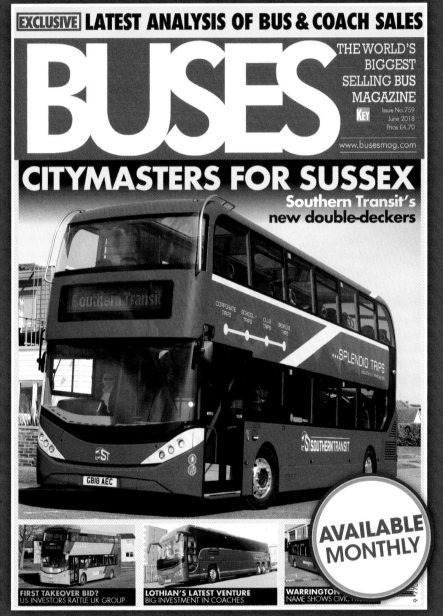

EXCLUSIVE **LATEST ANALYSIS OF BUS & COACH SALES**

## BUSES
THE WORLD'S BIGGEST SELLING BUS MAGAZINE
Issue No.759
June 2018
Price £4.70
www.busesmag.com

## CITYMASTERS FOR SUSSEX
Southern Transit's new double-deckers

AVAILABLE MONTHLY

FIRST TAKEOVER BID?
US INVESTORS RATTLE UK GROUP

LOTHIAN'S LATEST VENTURE
BIG INVESTMENT IN COACHES

WARRINGTON
NAME SHOWS CIVIC

---

## FOR LATEST SUBSCRIPTION DEALS VISIT: www.busesmag.com

## ALSO AVAILABLE IN DIGITAL FORMAT:

DOWNLOAD NOW

**FREE APP**
with sample issue
IN APP ISSUES £3.99

SEARCH BUSES

AVAILABLE FROM:

 Available on **BlackBerry**

 Available on **kindle** fire

 Available on PC, Mac & Windows 10

 Available on **iTunes**

 Available on the **App Store**

 Available on **Google play**

Available on PC, Mac, Blackberry, Windows 10 and kindle fire from  pocketmags.com

# The reshaping plan

*In 1968, London Transport began implementing a change to shorter suburban routes that fed into key interchange points. It came to be considered a failure, yet similar ideas are once again being proposed for the 2020s and beyond.*

Following a boom in the early postwar years, the number of passengers using London's buses began to fall in 1952, with the rate of loss accelerating rapidly after the seven-week drivers' strike in 1958 (see p14).

While part of this decline was down to a reduction in London's population, which fell from 8.2million in 1951 to 6.6million 30 years later, much of it was driven by increased car ownership and changes in lifestyle. The spread of television, for example, meant that fewer leisure trips were taken to the cinema.

Initially, London Transport responded to these losses by simply reducing service levels as a way of controlling costs, although this made the remaining services even less attractive and so hastened the decline.

A more radical move was the adoption of driver-only operation of certain routes. This was employed to a limited, but growing degree in the Country Area, but all Central Area routes had been operated by a driver and conductor since withdrawal of the 20-seat Leyland Cubs in 1949.

Negotiations with the trades unions were protracted and it was not until November 1964 that the first three red routes — all operated with RF-class AEC Regal IV single-deckers — lost their conductors. It took just

operated by 'standee' vehicles in which most passengers would stand rather than sit, as these would hold more passengers than conventional seated buses. Other approaches that were rejected included radial suburban routes feeding into a separate central network at dedicated interchanges and the adoption of flat fares.

Poor labour relations in the early 1960s, culminating in an overtime ban imposed in late October 1963, had an adverse impact on service reliability and drove more passengers away from London's buses.

### Phelps-Brown and the AEC Merlin

In November 1963, the Conservative government set up a committee of inquiry, chaired by Prof Henry Phelps-Brown of the London School of Economics. His remit was to review the pay and conditions of bus drivers and conductors in light of manpower requirements and working and operating conditions in London traffic.

In making its report, the committee was instructed to pay due regard to the possibilities of increasing the efficiency of London Transport's road services. It produced an interim report on 12 December recommending new rates of pay, which was rapidly implemented,

leading to the ending of the overtime ban.

The final report was published in June 1964 and recommended that bus workers' pay be linked to the earnings of skilled and semi-skilled workers in London. In return, staff were expected to agree to the extension of driver-only operation and experimental operation of both large standee single-deckers and front-entrance double-deckers.

Although the unions accepted much of the report, areas of disagreement with London Transport led to further industrial action.

Shortly afterwards, London Transport ordered 50 Park Royal-bodied Leyland Atlanteans (class XA) for use in the Central Area and eight similar Daimler Fleetlines (class XF) for the Country Area. These were slightly modified versions of vehicles already built for many bus fleets outside London.

Although the Atlanteans were to be used with conductors, the Fleetlines had gates fitted to the staircase that allowed the top deck to be closed in the off-peak period for driver-only operation.

Later in 1964, six 36ft AEC Merlin rear-engined standee single-deckers were ordered for a new limited stop route linking Victoria and Marble Arch. This was introduced in April 1966 as Red Arrow route 500 and

seven years for all single-deck routes to follow suit.

This may have been little more than tinkering around the edges, but plans for a radical overhaul of London's bus services had been considered from the mid-1950s, when the Chambers committee was set up to find ways of reducing costs and ascertaining what practical measures could be taken in order to secure greater efficiency or economies. This reported in 1955 but only made limited recommendations for change.

It appeared to rule out driver-only operation in much of London, citing the impact on traffic of slower boarding times, but did suggest that special services be introduced in the peak hours to cater for the heaviest traffic flows, such as those to and from the mainline railway termini.

These, it said, would be

**BELOW: Two preserved examples of buses that London Transport bought for the reshaping plan. AEC Merlin MBA582 represents the Red Arrow fleet operated in central London, while DMS1 behind was the first of 2,646 Fleetlines. This carries the Londoner name used briefly by London Transport.**

operated with a flat fare. A further seven similar buses, but fully seated, were ordered for the Country Area, although all except one ultimately entered service on Red Arrow services.

Following the success of the first Red Arrow route, London Transport set out to develop its reshaping plan, which was launched in September 1966 and was implemented from 1968.

Described as a drastic recasting, the main features of what was expected to be a 10- to 15-year programme were:
● Introduction of driver-only operation to address staff shortages and costs
● Shortening of routes to improve reliability and ease scheduling
● Flat fare routes centred on outer hubs
● Long single-deckers in place of double-deckers

The plan envisaged that about 40 suburban centres would have flat fare networks of short-distance routes with fare collection using automated turnstiles. These satellite routes would be feeders to the Underground and trunk routes.

A new system of numbering was to be used for the networks, with prefix letters identifying the geographical location. The number of centres was reduced to 36 in the final plan. Suburban routes not suitable for flat

fare networks were to retain a graduated fare system and would gradually be converted to driver-only single-deckers.

At the same time, plans were announced to purchase 650 large (36ft) single-deckers for delivery in 1968/69, of which 108 would go to the Country Area. As with the experimental buses, these would be AEC Merlins, a model that the manufacturer called the Swift when sold everywhere else.

The experimental buses had bodywork built in Hampshire by Strachans (pronounced 'Strawns') but these would all be built in Birmingham by Metro-Cammell Weymann.

The original plan was that the principal trunk routes between the suburbs and central London would remain operated in the medium term by rear-entrance double-deckers with conductors. Indeed, the last Routemasters arrived in early 1968.

## The first phase

The first phase of the plan took effect on 7 September 1968. Seven additional Red Arrow services were introduced, numbered 501 to 507. They served Waterloo, Victoria, Liverpool Street, Charing Cross and Marylebone stations. Several double-deck routes that entered central London were shortened as a result.

A flat fare satellite network

of six routes (W1 to W6) was based on Wood Green, when conventional routes in the area were either withdrawn or shortened.

A major change of services in the Walthamstow area was based on a hub at Walthamstow Central station on the Victoria Line, which had opened the previous week. Seven new routes were created, and 19 existing ones altered. Of the 45 new driver-only Merlins introduced to the area, 15 were flat fare standee versions and 30 were one-door 50-seaters for routes with graduated fares.

The second phase followed in October 1968 and affected routes in south-east London. Although no new flat fare networks were created, some existing routes were altered or shortened and converted to driver-only operation.

One of these was the 108 (then Bromley by Bow-Blackheath) —see p90 for today's version — which lost its crew-operated RT double-deckers for Merlins. The change, however, was largely driven by the introduction of a height limit in the Blackwall Tunnel, through which it passed.

By late 1968 it was clear that many of the changes were unpopular with passengers and it was discovered that in most cases punctuality and reliability had worsened on the converted routes. This was largely because

it took passengers longer to board the Merlins as they were unfamiliar with the fare collection system, and also because the Merlins were too long to be able to pull into every bus stop, forcing them to block the road and slow the flow of all traffic.

Driver-only operation of double-deckers had been legalised in 1966 and an early adopter of them was Manchester City Transport whose general manager was the visionary Ralph Bennett. He oversaw the development of what became known as the Mancunian, a modern looking two-door double-deck body built on both Leyland Atlantean and Daimler Fleetline chassis, the first of which entered service in 1968.

Bennett joined the London Transport Board in September 1968 and it announced a plan to buy 17 Fleetlines with a body style modelled on the Mancunian for delivery in 1969. This became the DMS class, although Bennett tried to have it branded as the Londoner. The first did not arrive until late 1970, by which time a further 100 had been ordered.

Like most of the Merlins, these had front entrances and centre exits. The entrance doors were split into two flows, allowing passengers either to pay through self-service turnstiles or pay the driver. It was also decided that

future single-deck orders would be for the more manoeuvrable 33ft version of the AEC Swift, which had a smaller and less powerful engine.

Despite these changes in approach, further conversions took place during 1969 using the longer Merlins.

In November 1969, route 233 linking Croydon and the housing estate at Roundshaw became the first driver-only double-deck route in London, using some of the XA-class Atlanteans as well as FRM1, a unique prototype rear-engined Routemaster that was built in 1966.

In January 1970, some of the Atlanteans were used for new Peckham circular route P3 while in April further examples were used on new routes C1 to C4, which replaced the previous Routemaster-operated express journeys on route 130 between Croydon and New Addington. These XAs were fitted with Johnson fareboxes.

The first of the shorter Swifts also began to enter service in 1970 and were used largely to convert crew-operated double-deck routes to driver-only operation.

Further examples followed, but with the first DMSs entering service in January 1971, London Transport concluded that its future deliveries would be double-deck.

## Routemaster reprieved

In 1972, following reliability problems with services converted to driver-only operation and flat fare, London Transport reconsidered whether it should continue to remove conductors from busy routes, particularly in central London.

It concluded that this was no longer practical, as boarding times would more than double, leading to longer journey times.

Under the original reshaping plan, the Routemaster fleet was due to be withdrawn from 1975, but it was now decided to continue their use indefinitely, and some of the new DMS double-deckers would now also be crew operated.

This effectively marked the end of the bus reshaping plan as originally conceived, although some more routes were changed over to driver-only operation during the 1970s. At the time, this was known as one-man operation, abbreviated to OMO, but in 1974 Jill Viner became the first female bus driver in London, leading to a change of terminology to OPO or one-person operation.

The longer boarding times associated with driver-only buses continued to hamper their wider application and London Transport continued to experiment with ways of speeding up this process.

**ABOVE: DMS435, a Daimler Fleetline with Park Royal body, near Aldenham Works on a route converted from single-deckers to double-deckers in 1972. Most Fleetlines were disposed of early, helping prolong the London career of the legendary Routemaster.**
TONY WILSON

Solutions considered included the Multiride scheme trialled in Havering (see p104) and the Autocheck system that employed magnetically-coded tickets similar to those used then on the Underground.

All proved unreliable, expensive to run and unpopular and the split entrance arrangements were abandoned in May 1979.

A partial solution was to coarsen the fares scale to values that were easy to pay using the minimum number of coins, thus reducing the need to give change.

Political issues, as well as the realisation that conversion of the busiest crew-operated routes would not be economically worthwhile within existing technical and operational constraints, meant that the process of converting routes to driver-only operation slowed down.

### Flat fares

In April 1981, London Transport introduced a flat suburban fare of 25p, marketed as Fare Deal, to simply the fares structure and speed up boarding. More dramatic change followed that October when the Fares Fair scheme was introduced.

This was the result of a manifesto commitment by the Labour Party, which had won control of the Greater London Council earlier in the year and had pledged to subsidise a big reduction in bus and Underground fares. This introduced fare zones across London, with graduated fares

determined by the number of zones crossed.

Following a legal challenge by the Conservative-led London Borough of Bromley, the scheme was ruled unlawful and, as a result, fares more than doubled from March 1982.

Passenger numbers fell dramatically, leading London Transport to reduce costs as rapidly as possible. An immediate consequence was that conversions of routes to driver-only operation resumed and withdrawal began of Routemasters, which by then were between 14 and 24 years old. By the end of the decade, they were largely confined to routes running through the West End.

Although the reshaping plan as such disappeared, London's bus network continued to change, with a particular desire to split longer routes into shorter sections less vulnerable to delays caused by traffic congestion. Many of these routes were similar to some of the local satellite routes conceived under the reshaping plan.

Ultimately the most successful method of speeding-up bus boarding was to encourage pre-purchase of travel from outlets such as newsagents. Although bus passes had been available for some time, it was the launch of the Capitalcard in 1985 that really encouraged off-bus ticketing.

This was followed shortly after, and ultimately superseded by the Travelcard, developed in conjunction with British Rail's Network SouthEast business to provide a ticket that covered all road and rail services in Greater London.

In January 2000 London's buses adopted two fare zones, with journeys entirely in the outer zone costing 70p and those within the central zone £1. The range of off-bus tickets was increased with the introduction of Saver tickets which provided for the purchase, in advance, of six tickets that gave a slight discount on the cash fare.

Electronic smartcard ticketing began to be developed in the 1980s, and in the early 1990s it had reached a point where practical trials were possible, which led subsequently to development of the Oyster card that has, since 2003, become the foundation for Transport for London's multi-modal ticketing system. In 2004 the fares system was further simplified with a single flat fare across the network. This speeded up the process of boarding considerably and helped pave the way for the final conversion of the bus network to driver-only operation in December 2005.

More recently, mayor Sadiq Khan's Hopper fare has allowed passengers to make multiple changes of bus within an hour without paying an additional fare.

### Turning full circle?

Between 2002 and 2011, many of London's busiest routes were operated by articulated single-deckers, popularly known as bendybuses. Although disliked by many, they proved to be effective people movers with three doors and cashless operation.

Cashless operation was subsequently rolled out across the West End, initially with self-service ticket machines at bus stops. By 2014, cash fares only accounted for around 1% of journeys, a change assisted by the acceptance of contactless

**ABOVE: Mercedes-Benz Citaro bendybus MAL3 in the Go-Ahead fleet crossing Lambeth Bridge on Red Arrow service 507.**

This year sees the opening of the Elizabeth Line, which will increase the capacity of London's rail network by around 10%. This line will provide a key east-west link across London and beyond and many people in inner and outer London are expected to use a bus to reach it.

Transport hubs will be created at Elizabeth Line stations in a move that echoes the changes brought in to coincide with the opening of the Victoria Line in 1968. The wheel appears to have turned full circle.

However, there are far more buses today. At the end of 1967, London Transport's Central Area bus fleet numbered 5,911, of which fewer than 200 were single-deck. Today, of just over 9,500 buses in London, more than a quarter are single-deck.

One thing that has changed is the acceptability of longer vehicles. The manoeuvrability of Merlins may have been criticised, but at 36ft 10in, the New Routemaster double-decker — of which there are 1,000 — is longer and seems able to operate through the heart of London without difficulty. Even longer three-axle double-deckers are used on sightseeing tours in central London and Transport for London is to trial such buses on its services too. ● **ML**

**ABOVE: BYD/ Alexander Dennis Enviro200EV electric single-deckers — at 12m (39ft 4in) they are more than 3ft longer than the Merlins — operate today's two surviving Red Arrow services. This is SEe24 in the Go-Ahead fleet.** GAVIN BOOTH

**RIGHT: New Routemasters also are nearly a foot longer than the supposedly cumbersome Merlins. Go-Ahead-operated LT942 is about to negotiate a tight turn on East London Transit route EL3 in Barking.**

payment cards, and the decision was taken to make the entire bus network cashless.

The long-term decline in bus passenger numbers was finally arrested in 2000. Many factors contributed to this including an increase in London's population and significant enhancements to bus services in the early years of the century. More recently, numbers have begun to decline, falling by over 6% since 2014, partly because lifestyle changes mean many people travel less often.

This, combined with increasing financial pressures, has led to demands for a review of the capital's bus network. In 2017 the Greater London Assembly's transport committee report *London's Bus Network* made several recommendations including moving towards a more efficient network design based on feeder and trunk routes, an approach not that dissimilar to the vision of the reshaping plan half a century earlier. It also suggested an increase in orbital routes and express buses.

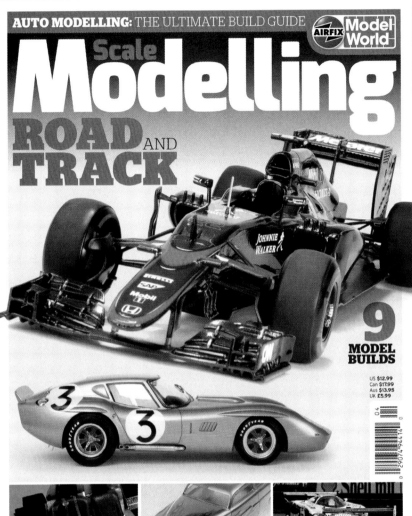

# Route 108

(the current southbound bore was opened in 1967).

Before the war, NS and STL double-deckers with specially adapted roofs were acquired in order to fit through the curved cross-section of the tunnel. Then in 1952 the roadway was lowered, and it was possible to put standard RT double-deckers on the service. However, the surface was raised again in the mid-1960s to increase the width by bringing it closer to the centre line, so double-deckers disappeared from the route.

Not surprisingly, extensive peak-hour congestion in the tunnel can play havoc with timetables, and is said to make the 108 London's most unpredictable route – though in fairness, during our visit it ran like clockwork.

Longer-term tunnel closures are another matter; from 2010 the southbound bore saw repeated evening and overnight closures for repair, and late evening services on the 108 had to be run in two parts – north of the river between Stratford

and Canning Town, and south of the river between North Greenwich and Lewisham.

The Canning Town diversion became a regular feature of the route, and curiously it was still shown on Transport for London's online route map when I checked it in spring 2018, though the stops were no longer served.

During the early days of bus privatisation in the 1990s, the 108 saw a succession of colourful liveries as the route was allocated to Boro'line Maidstone (blue and yellow), then Kentish Bus (maroon and cream), then Harris Bus (blue and green). When Harris failed, TfL took over the route with its own subsidiary East Thames Buses. Go-Ahead bought East Thames in 2009 and has retained the route since then.

Mercedes-Benz Citaros were the order of the day when I sampled the route. Although nine years old, they were smartly turned out – mostly in London's current overall red, but some featuring Go-Ahead's former grey skirt. However, having been cascaded from central London Red Arrow routes, some still

**BELOW: Mercedes-Benz Citaro MEC30 emerging from the northern portal of the Blackwall Tunnel.**

At first sight, there is something contradictory about north-south route 108 between Stratford and Lewisham. It is a high-intensity 11mile service with departures every 8 to 11min, yet it is operated by single-deckers.

The explanation is that it runs under the River Thames through the Blackwall Tunnel, and the headroom in the original northbound tunnel bore is insufficient to accommodate double-deckers.

The 108 is one of the oldest routes in London, having been launched in 1914. The original Blackwall Tunnel had already been open for 17 years by then

had large, empty standee areas forward of the central doorway, and consequently very few seats: scarcely an ideal arrangement for such a long route. Some also lacked a full destination display, showing only the route number. In these cases the final destination was shown neatly in a subsidiary display at the bottom of the windscreen.

A pair of Spanish-built Irizar i2e all-electric buses dating from 2015 were also cascaded from Red Arrow routes to the 108 in late 2016, though there was no sign of either when I rode the route. The only other performer I saw was a slightly tired-looking Alexander Dennis Enviro200.

There have been numerous changes to the route over the years, but its general axis has been maintained, and the tunnel has always played a part in it. These days the northern terminus is at Stratford International railway station, which falls within the development area surrounding the Olympic Park. Despite its name, no international trains serve the station, though it lies on the Channel Tunnel railway.

A branch of the Docklands Light Railway also terminates here – and offers a much quicker journey to Lewisham than the bus. But probably not many travellers would consider using the 108 for the whole trip.

We follow the route south from Stratford, starting among the gleaming new glass and metal offices and apartment blocks that are still being built following the massive pre-Olympic regeneration of the area. Passing the main Stratford station and Westfield shopping centre, we loop round close to the Olympic stadium (now home to West Ham football club) and the London Aquatic Centre, then continue on to the High Street, which forms part of the A11.

Skyscraper developments make this part of Stratford look like a mini-city, though there's a curious lack of people around to give the area a human scale.

Crossing the A12 dual carriageway under the shadow

**TOP LEFT & BELOW:** Contrasting interiors of route 108 Citaros, with and without additional seating in the front section.

**LEFT: Docklands Light Railway at Stratford International —** the quick way to Lewisham.

**BELOW:** Part of the Olympic Park and West Ham United stadium.

**ABOVE: Colourful skyscraper living in the mini-city that is modern Stratford.**

**RIGHT: Alexander Dennis Enviro200 providing vehicular variety on the 108.**

Not far along, we leave the A13 to loop down to the southbound A12, which here is carried in an underpass towards the Blackwall Tunnel portal. A couple of minutes later we are emerging south of the river on the Greenwich peninsula and forking left to make our way back north to the O2 arena and North Greenwich bus and Underground stations.

The terrain here is not unlike that at Stratford – excitingly futuristic, but with undeveloped patches where nothing much seems to be happening. However, the busy bus station radiates modern efficiency, and the mature piazza fronting the squat white dome of the O2 stadium forms a pleasant environment for visitors and office workers on their lunch break. Curious metal sculptures depicting various items of women's clothing were on display during my visit.

Overhead, there are glimpses

of the Bow flyover, the route continues a short way towards central London, then makes an abrupt left turn into Campbell Road, which seems too narrow to be part of a bus route. This takes us south for over a mile through an aspirational mixed landscape of residential, office and commercial development and converted warehousing. Then it's a left turn eastward on to East India Dock Road, a broad thoroughfare that forms part of the A13 – London's principal escape route to the east.

**ABOVE CENTRE: Citaro MEC3, with destination displayed behind the windscreen, on the Olympic Park loop.**

**TOP RIGHT: The location spelt out beneath the Bow flyover.**

**BELOW RIGHT: Langdon Park DLR station, close to Chrisp Street on which the 108 offers a less direct journey between Stratford and Lewisham.**

**LEFT: Following a German touring coach through the Blackwall Tunnel.**

of the cable cars of Emirates Air Line, which crosses the Thames from here to Royal Victoria Dock, and which – despite its name – is actually operated by Transport for London. And is a service of cable cars, not aeroplanes.

**ABOVE: The O2 arena, built in 1999 as the Millennium Dome.**

**RIGHT: Citaro MEC6 at Blackheath station.**

The 108 now heads south past the greenery of the Millennium Peninsula Ecology Park and the colourful dwellings of the Millennium Village – a modern development of low energy-use dwellings, and part of a broader government-inspired regeneration project.

Weaving under the A2 dual carriageway, we enter a very different world of upmarket Victorian houses as we climb through the Vanbrugh Park area towards Blackheath. At the top of the hill we emerge into a quaint area with a triangular village green called Batley Park. The spot is known colloquially as Blackheath Royal Standard after a large pub on one corner.

Continuing along the elegantly suburban Stratheaden Road, we cross Shooters Hill Road and strike out over Blackheath Common, a large open grassy expanse surrounded by distant Victorian housing. Then at the far side we descend into the pleasant and busy township of Blackheath proper.

From here we head east along further leafy suburban roads until we start to descend past terraced housing into the busy urban centre of Lewisham.

The southern terminus of the 108 has recently been moved a short way northwards from Lewisham Centre, a major shopping complex, to Lewisham railway station, though during my visit all southbound buses still displayed 'Lewisham Shopping Centre' as their destination. ● **PR**

**ABOVE & BELOW:** Curious sculptures of women's clothing on display on Greenwich Peninsula.

**ABOVE:** Lewisham clock tower.

**FAR LEFT:** The Emirates Air Line.

**LEFT:** Blackheath Common.

# Guys go to Scotland

**When postwar deliveries allowed London Transport to dispose of non-standard wartime double-deckers at the start of the 1950s, 189 of them went north of the border where major rebuilds made many of them unrecognisable**

**ABOVE: London Transport Guy Arab II G171 operating from Barking garage around 1950. It has a Northern Counties body and was delivered in June 1945 around a month after the war ended in Europe. It went to Scotland in 1951, sold to Alexander's, and in 1961 became part of the Alexander (Fife) fleet.**

F. G. REYNOLDS

In 1939, London Transport was well on its way to having a standardised fleet of modern buses that had been built to its own highly individual and detailed specification.

London Transport had been formed just six years earlier in a move to bring the UK capital's bus, tram and sub-surface railways into common ownership. With roundly 6,500 motorbuses, 600 trolleybuses, 2,000 trams plus the railway companies that together formed the Underground, this was the world's largest urban transport operator.

With such large fleets,

standardisation is essential. So as quickly as London Transport was clearing out its inheritance of non-standard buses, it was designing new types that were suited to London conditions. This mainly meant double-deckers and with types developed by its predecessor, London General, as a base it placed around 2,600 of its STL type in service between 1933 and 1939. These were based on the AEC Regent chassis, built at Southall in west London and the close relationship with London Transport meant that AEC could justifiably claim — as it said in its advertising — to be Builders of London's Buses.

As the 1930s drew to a close,

against a backdrop of the threat of war with Germany, AEC and London Transport had developed the RT double-decker, a dramatic step forward both in mechanical and design terms, and the prototype was placed in service just weeks before war was declared; between 1939 and 1941 a further 150 were produced before the pressures of war led to a temporary halt in the production of 'prewar' types and a move by the government towards creating simple no-frills utility buses that would be allocated to bus operators throughout the UK on the basis of need.

Which is why London Transport found itself

**ABOVE: Stripped of their utility bodywork, the chassis of three former London Transport Guy Arabs sit in Edinburgh Corporation's Central garage awaiting work on the chassis before dispatch south for new bodies. From left to right, they are G215, G214 and G272, all of which were new in 1945.** IAN MACLEAN

**LEFT: Two of the ex-London Guys sit at Edinburgh Corporation's Shrubhill Works in the course of mid-life refurbishment, which included replacing the ornate Duple fronts with glassfibre Leyland-style fronts in line with much of the fleet. The original Guy radiators can be seen.** GAVIN BOOTH

accumulating a fleet of 435 fairly basic Guy Arab double-deckers between 1942 and 1946. Guy Motors, based in Wolverhampton, had not been a major player in the bus world but had gained a reputation for sturdy vehicles.

While London Transport's main bus suppliers, AEC and Leyland, were concentrating on other war work, Guy was authorised to build its rugged Arab chassis, to be fitted with bodywork to a strict specification that made the best use of scarce resources. So there were to be no curves, the minimum of opening windows, wooden slatted seats when other materials were not available, and a simple destination display at the front only.

The new utility Guys were in stark contrast to the flowing modern lines of the early RT types built only months earlier, but they were essential to keep London moving.

ABOVE: A 1953 Duple trade press advertisement highlighting the lightness of the bodywork. GAVIN BOOTH COLLECTION

ABOVE RIGHT: A posed press photograph of one of the first of Edinburgh's rebuilt and rebodied Guys with its driver and conductor inspecting the access to the engine. GAVIN BOOTH COLLECTION

RIGHT: Well-laden Guy 315 (former London Transport G377) in Princes Street, Edinburgh on a tram-replacement service, passes two of the remaining trams. It shows it as delivered, with non-opening side windows. JOHN FOZARD

### Less refined

The Guys definitely lacked the refinement of the later STL or the RT. They had the five-cylinder Gardner 5LW engine, a unit that urban operators like Birmingham and Manchester had been specifying in their double-deckers; London might have preferred the beefier six-cylinder Gardner 6LW, but these were typically allocated to operators with hilly terrain.

The Guys had sliding mesh or constant mesh gearboxes that tested London drivers who had become used to the preselector gearboxes that were better suited to intense urban conditions.

The London Guy Arabs were allocated to eight garages and performed impressively throughout the war and in the early postwar period, but it was inevitable that London Transport would want to sacrifice non-standard buses in favour of its in-house RT design.

When production of the postwar RT started up, it progressed with a vengeance.

Preserved Edinburgh 314 (based on London Transport G77 new in 1943), restored with its replica original front, at the Scottish Vintage Bus Museum. GAVIN BOOTH

From the first deliveries in mid-1947 to the end of 1949, more than 3,100 RT family buses had joined the London fleet – that's an average of three-and-a-half buses a day. By the time deliveries had ceased in 1954, the RT family of AECs and Leylands totalled just short of 7,000 buses – so it was clear that this impressive influx would allow older and non-standard buses to

be withdrawn from the fleet.

Withdrawal of the 435 utility Guy Arabs started in 1951 and was complete by early 1953. The newest examples were barely seven years old and although the bodywork was sometimes less than sturdy because unseasoned timber had been used in its construction, the rugged Arab chassis still had life in it and could appeal to operators in the UK looking for lower cost buses in these difficult postwar years when operators often had to take what they could get their hands on to replace time-served buses that in normal circumstances would have been replaced years before.

But there was a problem. London Transport had been taken into state ownership in 1948 and was now part of the British Transport Commission, formed to bring Britain's railways, road haulage and many major bus companies under public ownership. BTC had a strict edict that buses could not be sold where they could reappear on local bus work.

In essence, this was to prevent former BTC-owned buses competing with any BTC-controlled buses – and there were plenty of these. One answer was overseas sales, and London Guys were exported to various parts of Africa and to Belgium, the Canary Islands, Ceylon and

**LEFT: Edinburgh Guy 346 in its later years, with Leyland-style front end, heels over as it turns from York Place into North St Andrew Street. This chassis began life as London Transport G197.**
GAVIN BOOTH

**MIDDLE LEFT: Operating an Alexander's Perth city service was former London Transport G371, a Weymann-bodied Arab new in 1945 and sold to Alexander's in 1953 to become its RO646.**
ALASTAIR DOUGLAS

**BELOW: Most of London Transport's 'wartime' Guys were delivered in 1945, many after the end of hostilities, and the Northern Counties-bodies examples were to a relaxed utility specification with more rounded lines. New to London Transport in November 1945, G294 was sold to Alexander's in March 1953 to become its RO701 and was withdrawn in 1962. It was photographed on a Perth city service.**
R. F. MACK

Daimler COG6 and CVG6 models, Little's interest in Guys indicated a change in direction. His goal was to get the tramway replacement started before making the inevitable large-scale investment in brand new buses to replace the city's 370 trams.

Amos's intervention caused the top people at BTC to soften their stance and stipulated that the buses should be sold directly to Edinburgh for use on local bus work and should not be resold by the corporation.

What Moris Little wanted to do was to scrap the utility bodies, modernise the chassis and fit new modern-looking bodies. Edinburgh was developing a close interest in lightweight buses, following the tendency for most buses to become increasingly heavy.

The city had AEC double-deckers weighing exactly 8tons, and single-deckers that weighed in at over 7tons, with the inevitable effect on fuel consumption. His target was to produce double-deckers under 7tons and over the next few years he achieved this goal.

Early in 1952 Edinburgh Corporation engineers were given the choice of available London Guys and chose 60 that seemed most suitable for conversion. They were collected from London's Edgware garage in April and May of 1952 and driven north for conversion. The bodies were scrapped and the chassis modified at the front end; most utility Guys were built with a longer bonnet to accommodate either the 5LW or 6LW engines,

so on the shorter 5LW-engined examples the radiator was unnecessarily far forward.

Edinburgh engineers shortened the chassis and mounted the radiator immediately in front of the engine and in doing so Edinburgh needed to allocate new chassis numbers. The new chassis numbers reflected the year of conversion and the fleetnumber of the bus, so the Guy chassis on buses nos.301-60 became 195201-60. The chassis were also widened from 7ft 6in to the now-legal 8ft.

## Duple bodywork

For bodywork, Edinburgh turned to Duple, based in Hendon in London and best known for its luxury coaches. Edinburgh's only previous Duple bodies were 29-seat Vista coaches on Bedford OWB and OB chassis. Duple had built double-deckers in the postwar period and the general design would follow the lines of these but with an emphasis on low overall weight.

This too was the era when exposed radiators (like on the London RT) were deemed to be old fashioned and new look 'tin' fronts, hiding the radiator, were in vogue. Edinburgh and Duple came up with a novel design that looked at first glance like the full fronts favoured by a few operators but in fact what would have been the nearside windscreen was actually simply an aperture, with a further aperture for engine access above the front nearside wheel. The lower front was a rather flashy one with brightwork that announced to all observers that this was definitely not a utility bus.

Duple built the pre-production prototype and the second one at Hendon, but the other 58 received lower deck shells at Hendon before transfer to Duple's recently acquired company, Nudd Bros & Lockyer, at Kegworth in Leicestershire where the bodies were completed.

Edinburgh had bought the chassis for the theoretical scrap value of £250 each, with bodies

**ABOVE: Former London Transport G252 with Northern Counties bodywork receives attention at Western SMT's Cumnock depot.**
GAVIN BOOTH

Yugoslavia. But to the frustration of UK operators, not to the home market.

## Acting for Edinburgh

This stalemate was broken by James Amos, chairman of the Scottish Bus Group, itself state-owned in BTC control. While its companies could – and did – buy former London Guys, Amos was also negotiating on behalf of Moris Little, transport manager at Edinburgh Corporation, who was looking for low cost lightweight buses to start full-scale replacement of the city's tramway network.

Edinburgh Corporation had been allocated six utility Guy double-deckers in 1943 and went on to buy a further 42 between 1945 and 1951 – all with the bigger Gardner 6LW engine. Although Edinburgh's double-deck preference for many years had been the 6LW-engined

It was based on the oldest chassis, that of London G77 new in June 1943, and during its Edinburgh existence, in 1963, it was the only one to gain a beefier Gardner 6LW engine, which necessitated an extension to the front end.

By this time the front ends on all 60 had changed. The ornate Duple front had given way to a simpler glassfibre Leyland-style front, in the interests of easy replacement in the event of accident damage. During its subsequent 49 years in preservation, 314 has been re-engined with the more typical 5LW engine and its original ornate front end has been accurately recreated.

## SBG purchases them too

Edinburgh was not the only Scottish operator to benefit from the sale of the London Guys.

that cost £1,700 each; add in around £600 for overhauling and modernising the chassis and Edinburgh got 60 serviceable double-deckers for £2,550 each, when new ones were topping £4,000 each.

The buses were delivered to Edinburgh over the seven months between late 1952 and July 1953 and went into service on tram replacement routes. They were an essential part of the city fleet working front-line duties well into the 1960s, with

the first withdrawals in 1967; the last examples left the fleet in 1969.

The 17 years in Edinburgh service testified to the Guy/ Duple combination – and at least some of the chassis already had 10 years' London service under their belt before they came to Edinburgh.

True to its word, Edinburgh sold 59 of the 60 Guys to dealers for scrapping. The 60th bus survived to be preserved. No.314 was interesting in several ways.

Alexander blue and cream.

Twenty-seven of them survived the split of Alexander into three companies in 1961 – 17 with Alexander (Midland) and 10 with Alexander (Fife); the last of the Fife examples were withdrawn in 1964. All the Alexander examples held on to their original Northern Counties, Park Royal or Weymann bodies.

The typical Scottish Bus Group double-decker was built to a height of roughly 13ft 6in (4.1m) to cope with low bridges and, in several cases, low depot entrances. Most urban buses around Britain were 14ft 6in high (4.4m), so SBG operators could only use the full-height London Guys in certain areas. The Alexander company concentrated them on those depots where there was no problem with bridges – or depots.

Western SMT had different ideas. It took 65 of the Guys and although 28 ran with their original bodies – mostly metal-framed Northern Counties ones – the rest received new or secondhand bodies. Alexander provided new lowbridge bodies for 19 of them and eight received 1947 lowbridge bodies by Croft of Glasgow, which had previously been used to rebody

prewar Leyland Titans.

The remaining 10 were extensively rebuilt with new Northern Counties lowbridge bodies and Birmingham-style tin fronts that meant they were largely indistinguishable from brand-new Guy Arab IVs entering the Western fleet at the same time.

An even more substantial rebuild was carried out on 23 former London Guys, which emerged from the Scottish Omnibuses coachworks at Marine Gardens, Edinburgh as single-deckers. In 1951, Scottish Omnibuses had received eight London Guys and initially operated them as double-deckers. Similarly, the new Highland Omnibuses company ran two as double-deckers from 1952.

These 10 plus another 13 lost their original double-deck bodies, the chassis were lengthened to accommodate new 30ft-long bodies and they emerged as 39-seat single-deckers between 1952 and 1954. All but five went to Highland Omnibuses where they lasted in service for up to 13 years; the other five went into Scottish Omnibuses' own fleet in 1954 for rural services in the Scottish Borders but lasted just seven years.

**ABOVE: The 10 London Guys rebuilt and rebodied by Northern Counties for Western SMT in 1954 were almost identical to new Arab IVs delivered to Western between 1953 and 1955. The chassis of Y1064 started life as London Transport G392 in 1945 and remained in service in Scotland until 1967. It was photographed in Paisley.** HARRY HAY

Always on the lookout for a bargain, several of the Scottish Bus Group's operating companies took London Guys and gave them extra life, sometimes – but not always – by rebodying them.

As the Scottish Bus Group was part of the British Transport Commission, there were no barriers to the purchase of London's cast-offs, so between 1951 and 1953 group companies bought 129 London Guys. At £185 each, these were bargains to gladden any Scottish accountant's heart.

Some were placed in service in Scotland virtually as received from London, notably with the giant W. Alexander company, which took 54, although not all were used in service. Of the 43 that were used, 32 were allocated to town services in Kirkcaldy and Perth and painted in the red town service livery. The others wore the more familiar

**In 1951 Scottish Omnibuses received eight London Guys and initially operated them as double-deckers before using them in 1953 as the basis for some of the homemade single-deckers. This Massey-bodied 1945 example, new to London Transport as G366, was photographed in Edinburgh's St Andrew Square in April 1953; the London red was over-painted in green while they ran as double-deckers.** J. C. GILLHAM

## RTs, Routemasters and Wright Gemini 2s

One other major Scottish bus fleet turned to London Transport in the 1950s for relatively young and inexpensive double-deckers. Dundee Corporation, working towards the final withdrawal of its tramway system, invested in 10 early postwar STL-class AEC Regent IIs with Weymann bodies and 30 Cravens-bodied AEC Regent RT types in 1956.

London Transport's 120 Cravens RTs were non-standard in an increasingly standardised fleet and were sold in 1956/57 when they were barely seven years old. Others went to Scottish independent operators and when

the mainstream RTs and RTLs were withdrawn some years later, Scottish companies were equally quick to snap them up.

It looked as if London as a source of secondhand double-deckers might have dried up until Western Scottish bought 33 fairly new Daimler Fleetlines, while Highland Scottish bought two former London Fleetlines third hand. The most unexpected purchase of former London buses by Scottish Bus Group companies followed between 1985 and 1988 when the group's Clydeside, Kelvin and Strathtay companies bought 168 Routemasters at the time of bus service deregulation. These iconic but

elderly buses were used on competitive services in the initial post-deregulation skirmishes but had been withdrawn by 1990.

History vaguely repeated itself in 2018 when Lothian Buses, successor to Edinburgh Corporation Transport, bought 50 six-year old Wright Eclipse Gemini 2-bodied Volvo B9TLs from London to speed withdrawal of older double-deckers and increase the proportion of low-emission buses in its fleet. All were new to FirstGroup, two coming after service with Tower Transit and 48 from Metroline.

They have been heavily rebuilt and refurbished, losing their centre doors and gaining new seats, and like the 60 Guys have also been given new registrations that disguise their age.

Sixty-five years after the former London Guys helped Edinburgh Corporation embark on its tramway replacement programme, London is still providing buses for operators throughout the UK. ● **GB**

**LEFT: Five of the 23 30ft-long single-deckers converted by Scottish Omnibuses from former London Transport Guy Arab double-deckers remained with Scottish Omnibuses, while the rest went to Highland Omnibuses. This one was photographed in Edinburgh later in its life.** JASPER PETTIE COLLECTION

**BELOW: History turns full circle. Lothian Buses 1002, one of two Wright Eclipse Gemini-bodied Volvo B9TLs bought ex-Tower Transit in London in 2018, on Edinburgh's Princes Street where trams returned in 2014, 58 years after the city's previous generation tram system closed, hastened on its way by the purchase of 60 ex-London Guys.** GAVIN BOOTH

# Romford

*Built as part of London Transport's postwar expansion plans, North Street garage is one of six bases used by Stagecoach East London*

**ABOVE: Aerial view of Romford garage.** GOOGLE

Sharply increased bus patronage in the years immediately after World War 2 led London Transport to formulate ambitious plans to redevelop existing garages and build new ones to cater for growth and relieve pressure on overcrowded facilities.

One of these is at North Street in Romford, which opened its doors in August 1953 and was intended to relieve pressure on the garages at Hornchurch, Barking and Seven Kings, all of which were operating beyond capacity. The area was also expected to see significant growth in services as a result

of the building, by the London County Council, of a large housing estate at Harold Wood.

When first opened, it had a peak requirement of 67 buses running on nine routes, but within five years this had increased to 99. The garage was initially described as North Street, with code letters NS, to differentiate it from the now closed Green Line garage in Romford.

In October 1975 Romford gained an allocation of 13 ex-British Airways Routemasters, with forward entrances and folding doors, which were used for around 11 months on route 175 until they were redeployed for driver training.

In February 1978 London Transport launched Multiride tickets in the Havering area in a bid to speed up boarding times on driver-only buses. The experiment covered several routes operated by Romford garage. Passengers could buy card tickets worth 10 units for 50p, which were then cancelled by being inserted into a slot once, twice or three times, depending upon distance travelled. Multiride journeys cost about half that of buying a separate ticket for each journey. The experiment was abandoned in February 1980.

In 1992 as a result of tendering losses it was proposed to close North Street, Seven Kings and

**ABOVE: Street level view of the garage in 1966.**
GERALD MEAD

Barking garages and replace them with a single site at Chadwell Heath. This plan did not come to fruition although Seven Kings garage did close in March 1993.

When London Buses established smaller subsidiaries for its bus operations, the garage came under the East London Bus & Coach Company, which was sold to Stagecoach in September 1994. In 2006, Stagecoach sold its London bus operations to Australia's Macquarie Bank for £263.6million, but reacquired the business in 2010 for £59.5million.

Today Romford provides buses for seven daytime routes under contract to Transport for London, plus a single vehicle for route 256 (Noak Hill-Hornchurch) and the night service on route 365 (South Hornchurch-Havering Park). Rainham garage operates the main daytime service on both routes.

## Strange case of the 86A

Although no London bus route carries a suffix to its route number today, this was not always the case. Romford and Stratford have been linked by buses carrying the number 86 since the early days of London Transport but for many years there was also an 86A.

The original 86 ran from Stratford Broadway along the old Roman's Great Road to Colchester as far as Brentwood. It was extended west to Mile End by December 1939 but was soon curtailed to run between Chadwell Heath and Brentwood, with occasional journeys reintroduced to Stratford shortly afterwards. These did not, however, last beyond 1941. The route was withdrawn in August 1958, one of the changes in the wake of the bus workers' strike earlier that year (see p14).

The 86A was another matter. For many years this was the main route linking Romford and Stratford. At its greatest extend it ran west to Mile End and east to Upminster. North Street, as then described, had a share in it from 1954, along with Upton Park, Seven Kings and Hornchurch, which have all

### Routes operated by Stagecoach, Romford garage

| Route | Vehicle type | Peak vehicle requirement | Contract start date |
| --- | --- | --- | --- |
| 86 (Stratford-Romford) N86 (Stratford-Harold Hill) | TransBus or Alexander Dennis Trident/ALX400 Alexander Dennis Enviro400 | 31 plus two from West Ham | 16 July 2016 |
| 247 (Barkingside-Romford) | TransBus or Alexander Dennis Trident/ALX400 | 11 | 24 March 2018 |
| 294 (Noak Hill-Havering Park) | Alexander Dennis Enviro400 MMC | 12 | 30 April 2016 |
| 296 (Ilford-Romford) 24hr Friday/Saturday | Alexander Dennis Enviro200 | 6 | 17 October 2015 |
| 496 (Harold Wood-Romford) | Alexander Dennis Enviro400 | 8 | 17 October 2015 |
| 498 (Brentwood-Romford) | Alexander Dennis Enviro400 | 6 | 27 June 2015 |
| 499 (Gallows Corner-Heath Park) | Alexander Dennis Enviro200 MMC | 7 | 27 June 2015 |

exception of one short-lived peak duty from Hornchurch garage, operation passed to the newly opened North Street in August 1953.

Although Seven Kings provided a partial allocation between 1986 and 1993, the route has been associated with North Street ever since. It took on its present route in 1993 when it was one of a few services in the area to receive Wright Handybus-bodied Dennis Dart single-deckers with East London Hoppa branding.

Low-floor single-deckers took their place in 1999 and it received double-deckers in 2004. These were 9.9m TransBus ALX400-bodied Tridents, a rarity in Stagecoach London's fleet where most Tridents are 10.8m long. They can be told apart as they have only one window between the front and centre doors.

In April 2017 the 247 was one of seven services in the Barkingside area to be included in a trial of route branding to see if this led to passenger growth. Several vehicles received yellow branding setting out the route and frequency of the service. Following award of a new contract in March 2018, newer Alexander Dennis Enviro400 double-deckers are being introduced.

In 1970 route 294 replaced

**ABOVE: RMA3, one of 13 former British Airways Routemasters operated from North Street on route 175 in 1975/76. They had been built for the service linking Heathrow Airport and the West London Air Terminal and lacked proper destination displays.**
TONY WILSON

**RIGHT: Alexander Dennis ALX400-bodied Trident 18453 leaving Stratford bus station for Romford on route 86.**

since closed. In 1959 the route took the then vacant number 86 and in 1963 the North Street allocation was withdrawn.

Tendering saw the route pass to East London in March 1993, by which time it had taken on its current termini. Operation transferred in its entirety to Romford following closure of Seven Kings garage. Four years later Bow garage gained a share, which was transferred to Stratford in 2001 with the remainder of the operation following in 2005.

The Stratford site was redeveloped as part of the

Olympic Park and its bus operations moved to a new garage at West Ham in 2008. Following retendering in 2009, operation transferred again to North Street although, since 2013, West Ham has also provided two vehicles.

### Back to double-deck
The present day route 247 (Romford-Barkingside) dates from 1992 when the 247A was renumbered as part of London Buses' policy of abolishing route suffixes. It was introduced in 1950, initially linking Collier Row and Harold Wood. With the

the outer sections of the 66 and 66A between Collier Row and Hornchurch, initially with RTs from North Street, which is the only garage to have operated the route. Conversion to driver-only operation followed a year later, using SMS-class AEC Swift single-deckers. The current route dates from 1986 and describes a U-shape from Noak Hill in the north-east, though Gidea Park and Romford to Havering Park in the north-west.

Route 296 (Ilford-Romford) is another result of the September 1982 reorganisation of London bus services and ran initially between Harold Wood and Romford using Leyland Titans from North Street. In 1987 it was altered to run between Harold Wood and Ilford via Romford, replacing routes 66A and 139. Tendering saw the route pass to Capital Citybus in October 1992.

In 2000 the Romford-Harold Hill section was passed to new service 496, operation of which was awarded to Stagecoach East London with vehicles allocated to North Street. The 296 retuned there in 2005 following a tender win and both routes have been operated from this site since then. A weekend night service was introduced in August 2016.

## In place of First Essex

In 2005, First Essex — formerly Eastern National — withdrew the section of route 351 (then Chelmsford-Romford) west of Brentwood, which had operated within Greater London under a London Local Services Agreement as an integral part of the bus network.

Transport for London replaced the withdrawn section and route 498 started running on 26 December, with operation initially contracted to Arriva Southern Counties. First Essex continued to run a Sunday service under contract to Essex County Council until August 2007.

Retendering transferred the route to First London in 2008, then to Go-Ahead Blue Triangle in June 2013 when Go-Ahead acquired First's Dagenham operation. Stagecoach won

**TOP LEFT:**
**Experimental branding, showing the main intermediate points on route 247, applied to Stagecoach 17981, one of the short length TransBus ALX400-bodied Tridents. TransBus International was the UK bus manufacturer acquired from receivership in 2004 and renamed Alexander Dennis.**
RICHARD GODFREY

**BELOW TOP LEFT:**
**TransBus ALX400-bodied 9.9m Trident 17989 in Harold Wood on route 294 when painted in the livery that Stagecoach was permitted to use before Transport for London insisted on 100% red buses on the network. The dark blue skirt and orange and blue swoops towards the rear were adapted from the group's standard livery outside London.**

**THIRD DOWN:**
**TransBus ALX400-bodied Trident 17979 in Romford on route 294 in 2014, designed Transport for London's Year of the Bus, with commemorative graphics on the panel behind the front wheel.**
PAUL GODDING

**BOTTOM:**
**Alexander Dennis Enviro200 36261 in Ilford on route 296.**

it in the next tender round, taking over in June 2015. It was operated initially with Tridents, but new Alexander Dennis Enviro400 MMCs were allocated to Romford, the first pure diesel-powered examples of this type — as opposed to hybrids — to be used in London.

Weekdays-only route 499 was introduced in July 1994, providing a link between Romford town centre and Whalebone Lane, largely in a one-way anticlockwise loop. The contract to provide the service was awarded to Stagecoach, which initially used a single bus, based at North Street.

In June 2002 operation transferred to First London, the service was extended to Gallows Corner and run seven days a week. Retendering in 2009 saw Arriva take over until a further change of operator in June 2015 brought the route back to Romford with a requirement for new buses, the first Alexander Dennis Enviro200 MMC single-deckers in London.

In September 2018 it will start operating route 193 (Romford-County Park Estate), which has been won on retendering from Go-Ahead's Blue Triangle.

The 193 was among the first London bus routes offered out to tender in July 1985. Eastern National won it then, initially using ECW-bodied Bristol VRT double-deckers although Mercedes-Benz minibuses

replaced these the following year. Services have since been provided by Thamesway, First Essex, First London and now Blue Triangle, but these changes in operator have been a result of restructuring or takeover of the incumbent operator rather than the tendering process.

Sixty-five years after it first opened, Romford garage is

once again in an area where there is significant new housing development and its buses operate in the sort of suburban area in which Transport fro London hopes to increase bus service provision. In addition, changes associated with the opening of the Elizabeth Line are likely to result in new bus links feeding traffic into railheads. ● **ML**

# Route X26

Heathrow Central **X26**

**BELOW: WVL340,
a Wright Eclipse
Gemini 2-bodied
Volvo B9TL
refurbished
for route X26,
leaving East
Croydon alongside
the tracks and
platform for
Tramlink.**

If you wanted to travel from Croydon in south London to Heathrow airport in the west, would you go by bus? You certainly could, using the X26. This remarkable service runs every half hour, using double-deckers with a special luggage pen in the lower saloon for the benefit of flight passengers.

The X26 was launched in its present form in 2005, but is based on Green Line coach service 725 (later 726), which dates back to the early 1950s. As with so many London routes, it was once much longer, starting from Gravesend in Kent and continuing to Windsor in Berkshire; but even in its current form, at 23.7miles it is the capital's longest daytime red bus route. In order to help minimise delays over such a long route, it is a limited-stop service; hence the X for 'express' in the route number.

Even during its relatively short life as the X26, the service has seen various changes of operator and vehicle type. Initially it was run by Go-Ahead subsidiary Metrobus with Scania OmniCity single-deckers, then Quality Line took over. Demand grew, and double-deckers were drafted in.

Then when Go-Ahead London General won the contract in 2017, it refurbished a batch of nine-year-old double-deckers for the route. These are Volvo B9TLs with Wright Eclipse Gemini 2 bodywork, and were previously used on the group's East London Transit operation. They have been replaced there by New Routemasters.

The refurbishment job is impressive (see p46). Externally the buses gleam, and inside everything looks fresh and new, from the relatively unblemished flooring to the grab rails and stanchions, which are orange rather than London General's usual yellow. They are single-door buses, which helps avoid too much loss of seating to accommodate the offside luggage racks. Nevertheless, there are only 17 seats on the lower deck.

When I sampled the route during April's brief heatwave, I was keen to see whether in fact it was used by airport-bound travellers who needed the luggage racks. In my admittedly limited experience the answer was yes, but only up to a point. People really did board with suitcases – apparently business users, moreover, who might have been expected to be using a taxi or some other supposedly more upmarket means of transport. But they appeared to be in a minority.

By far the majority of passengers boarded and alighted at intermediate stops. It soon became apparent that many of them were not waiting specifically for an X26 (perhaps unlikely with a half-hourly service); they were simply using it as an alternative to other services running on the same parts of the route.

Whatever the users' reasons for travelling, the buses on the route were certainly busy all through the day, and on the final leg of our journey, from Teddington to Heathrow, there was standing

TOP LEFT: Bus stop publicity for the larger vehicles on the X26.

TOP RIGHT: Street-running Tramlink trams connect Croydon with Wimbledon, New Addington and Elmers End in part over tracks taken over from less frequent full-size trains.

LEFT: Renovation work on Croydon's Fairfield Halls, close to East Croydon station.

BELOW LEFT: A tram passes the Royal Hospital of the Holy Trinity in Croydon, founded in 1596 by Archbishop Whitgift.

BOTTOM: Whitgift's name also is commemorated by the major shopping centre between East and West Croydon.

room only.

We start our journey at Croydon, where the route has been tweaked over the years to serve both West and East Croydon railway stations. Croydon has the feel of a city in its own right, complete with its attractive Tramlink system. Admittedly, the celebrated Fairfield Halls concert venue looks dowdy, and much in need of the refurbishment it appears to be getting, but there is almost an air of aspirational chic these days about the street cafés in the main shopping area.

From here the X26 heads directly west along the A232. Almost the whole of the route is built up, but the suburban sprawl is interrupted by a succession of distinct villages and small towns. First comes the mixed residential and light industrial area of Waddon – though all we see of it is a complicated series of road junctions around Waddon station.

Next come Beddington and Wallington, but again we pass some distance from their central areas, and soon we're entering the elegant Carshalton village: quaint period buildings, and the picturesque Carshalton Ponds, divided by a causeway. You could alight here to search out the Hollywood Museum or the Grade II listed 18th century water tower, built to serve the nearby Carshalton House (now a school).

From here it's less than 2miles to Sutton, one of south London's bigger towns, and reputedly the fourth busiest shopping venue in the capital. The bus skirts

**ABOVE LEFT:**
**Carshalton Ponds,**
**where the X26**
**meets a Wright-**
**bodied Volvo of**
**Go-Ahead on**
**route 127 from**
**Totting Broadway**
**to Purley.**

**ABOVE RIGHT:**
**Sutton High**
**Street, once**
**served by two-way**
**buses and now**
**pedestrianised.**

**BELOW RIGHT:**
**Old pub and**
**direction signs**
**at the former**
**crossroads in the**
**centre of Sutton.**

the central area on the one-way system, pausing at the post office, but a striking landmark on the return journey is the gothic-style Trinity Church. Although completed only in 1907, it looks much older and is Grade II listed. Among distinctive features is its square tower with its tall fluted columns and its unusual 'crown and lantern' spire.

We head on west as far as Cheam. The crossroads at the centre of this village is characterised by distinctive inter-war buildings, some finished in mock-Tudor style. Although the look is not to everyone's taste, here it has an unexpected charm. Not far away, a noted tourist attraction is Nonsuch Park, part of a hunting ground used by Henry VIII.

Now we turn north, finally leaving the A232, and continue to North Cheam – a land of terraced houses that perhaps lacks the charm of Cheam itself. After further stretches of housing, we arrive at Worcester Park – yet another substantial south London township. Approaching the town centre, we pass an unusual performer on

the X26 – a Volvo B5LH hybrid with Wright Gemini 3 bodywork.

Worcester Park has a half-mile long main street, Central Road,

which winds gently down to the station. Although you won't see it from the bus, an intriguing development here is the Hamptons,

LEFT: The Grade II listed Trinity Church in Sutton, completed in 1907.

MIDDLE: Central Road descends through Worcester Park towards its railway station.

BOTTOM: WHV63, a Wright Gemini 3-bodied Volvo B5LH hybrid, entering North Cheam from Worcester Park.

a modern housing development built in distinctive North American 'colonial revival' style.

The next leg of our journey takes us close to, but not actually into, Old Malden. Instead, we cut past it to cross the A3 dual carriageway, skirting New Malden and making our way to the next big urban centre, Kingston. This is a significant retail venue for the whole area, and also a major confluence of traffic. Back in the 1970s the bus garage here was one of the last haunts of London Transport's

RF-class underfloor-engined AEC Regal IV single-deckers.

We cross the River Thames on the broad Kingston Bridge, then get almost our first taste of countryside as we pass allotments and parkland at Hampton Wick on our way to Teddington. Although Teddington Lock and Weir are well-known landmarks on the Thames, the town centre itself is some way from the river.

Boarding an X26 here at the beginning of the evening rush hour, we now have to endure a slow grind across complex junctions with Hounslow Road, Staines Road and the Great West Road. Unfortunately for us, the entire upper deck seems to be occupied by vociferous schoolboys on their way home. Standing downstairs adjacent to the luggage pen for half an hour, we have plenty of time to reflect on the limited seating, to listen to the relatively noisy diesel engine, and to wish the air conditioning was turned on.

Finally we arrive at Hatton Cross, on the fringe of Heathrow Airport. Most passengers leave the bus here;

just a few intrepid travellers stay on board as we embark on a circuitous route round the airport's perimeter road. It takes some minutes to make our way to the north side of the airport in order to reach the main terminals via the access tunnel under the runway.

The compact but orderly bus station adjacent to the passenger terminals is thronging with passengers as our bus pulls away and prepares to lay over in preparation for the long return trip to Croydon. ● **PR**

**LEFT:** Journey's end, as WVL336 unloads its passengers in the Central Bus Station before preparing to return to Croydon.

**BOTTOM LEFT:** Aircraft landing and taxiing, viewed from the top deck of an X26.

**BOTTOM RIGHT:** Some X26 passengers bring airline luggage.

# Bexley

*The only new garage built to accommodate any of London's huge trolleybus fleet, the one coded BX has had a chequered history of changes of operators as well as vehicles and even a two-year period when it was closed*

**ABOVE:
Aerial view of
Bexleyheath
garage.** GOOGLE

**BELOW: D2 class
trolleybus 432,
a 1937 Leyland
with Metro-
Cammell body, at
Bexleyheath depot
in the late 1950s.**
MICHAEL DFRYHURST

Bexleyheath garage — code BX today — was the only London Transport depot built new for its trolleybus network, although the Tram & Trolleybus Department always called it Bexley.

*Transport World* described this south-east London facility as a 'model home for trolleybuses… carefully planned throughout'. It opened on 10 November 1935 when trolleybuses replaced trams on routes 696 (Dartford-Welling-Woolwich) and 698 (Bexleyheath-Abbey Wood-Woolwich), which were separated from the rest of the trolleybus network.

These had originally been operated by Bexleyheath Urban District Council and Dartford Council, which merged their tramways during World War 1 to form the Bexley-Dartford Joint Tramways Committee.

The new depot was badly damaged twice by bombing in World War 2, first in an air raid on 7 November 1940 and again by a V1 flying bomb on 29 June 1944. The second incident caused significant damage, with 12 trolleybuses destroyed and 26 requiring replacement bodies.

The physical isolation of the Bexleyheath routes was one of the factors that caused its routes to be included in the first stage of London Transport's programme to replace trolleybuses with motorbuses, and on 4 March 1959 motorbus service 96 replaced the 696, while the 698 was replaced by extending the 229, which had operated hitherto between Orpington and Bexleyheath.

The plan then was for new Routemasters to replace all the trolleybuses, but delivery from AEC and Park Royal was running behind schedule, so Bexleyheath received RTs, made surplus by service cuts following the bus crews' strike the year before.

Fast forward to the introduction of route tendering in 1985 and London Buses was losing work to other operators. As the fleet reduced in size, it had more garages than it required, and in August 1986 Bexleyheath garage was closed with its routes reallocated to Plumstead, Catford and Sidcup. But the site was retained.

**Routes operated by Go-Ahead, Bexleyheath garage**

| Route | Vehicle type | Peak vehicle requirement | Contract start date |
|---|---|---|---|
| 89 (Lewisham-Slade Green) N89 (Lewisham-Erith) | Alexander Dennis Enviro400 | 15 | 21 Aug 2017 |
| 132 (Bexleyheath-North Greenwich) 24hr Friday/Saturday | Alexander Dennis Enviro400 | 15 | 1 Oct 2016 |
| 244 (Abbey Wood-Queen Elizabeth Hospital) | Alexander Dennis Enviro200 | 12 | 22 Jan 2011 |
| 486 (Bexleyheath-North Greenwich) 24hr Friday/Saturday | Alexander Dennis Enviro400 | 16 | 22 Feb 2014 |
| B11 (Thamesmead-Bexleyheath) | Alcxander Dennis Enviro200 | 7 | 22 Jan 2011 |
| B16 (Bexleyheath-Kidbrooke) | Alexander Dennis Enviro200 | 9 | 20 Jan 2018 |

By the late 1980s, such was the loss of work to other operators that London Buses began looking at ways to reduce costs. One was to establish low cost local operating units, starting with Kingston Bus in 1987.

Bexleybus was the fourth, starting operations from a reopened Bexleyheath garage on 16 January 1988 with 107 buses, including 28 new leased Northern Counties-bodied Leyland Olympians double-deckers that had been ordered by Greater Manchester Buses. Rather than the usual red, this fleet was blue and cream. The launch of the new operating unit, which was overseen by London Buses' Selkent subsidiary, prompted the closure of Sidcup garage.

Like some of the other low cost units, Bexleybus suffered from poor industrial relations and its services became unreliable. In a drive to improve reliability of its other 15 routes, in October 1998 London Transport transferred routes 422 (Bexley-Woolwich) and 492 (Sidcup-Dartford) to Boro'line Maidstone, owned by Maidstone Borough Council.

When Bexleybus lost contracts to operate nine of its routes to London Central in the next round of tendering, London Buses transferred the garage from Selkent to London Central to coincide with the start of the new contracts on 24 January 1991. That also was the end of the Bexleybus brand.

In September 1994 London Central became the fourth London Buses subsidiary to be sold in the privatisation programme. It was acquired by the Go-Ahead Group, which expanded in May 1996 to buy London General from the management team that had purchased it at privatisation. In 2017 all of Go-Ahead's London operations were placed under the London General operator licence, although separate fleetnames are still used.

The London tendering regime means that there is always a risk of garages losing work and in January 2018 three routes, equating to work for around 30 buses, were lost to Stagecoach Selkent and Arriva London. The garage currently operates six all-day routes for Transport for London. One of these runs 24hr a day while two provide a night service at the weekend. It provides buses for four schooldays-only services.

**LEFT: RTs and DMS-class Fleetlines at Bexleyheath garage in April 1977. One of the RTs has worked the 89, one of the routes still based there over 40 years later.** GERALD MEAD

### The much-altered 89

**ABOVE: Bexleybus 59, a Leyland National originally numbered LS294 in the main London Transport fleet, with an Iveco minibus behind.**
EAMONN KENTELL

**RIGHT: Bexleyheath-based E50, an Alexander Dennis Enviro400, in Blackheath.**

Like many of London's long established routes, the 89 has changed significantly over the years. Its initial route was from Plumstead via Lewisham to Bromley with some journeys extended to Westerham. By the outbreak of World War 2, its northern terminal point had moved to Welling and it was curtailed to run only between there and Lewisham in November 1939.

In 1963 it was extended from Welling to Eltham with part of the allocation transferred to Bexleyheath garage alongside buses from New Cross. By 1978 it was the last route at Bexleyheath to use RT double-deckers, but these were replaced by DMS-class Fleetlines from 22 April when all operations were transferred to Bexleyheath and the 89 was diverted to terminate at Slade Green instead of Eltham.

When Bexleyheath garage closed in 1986, operation of the 86 passed to New Cross until 1991 when some of its buses returned to Bexleyheath. The remainder of the operation followed in 2000 although New Cross operated some journeys between 2002 and 2005. Night service N89, between Trafalgar Square and Erith, began in June 2002.

Although it originally ran between Lewisham and Bexley with a Sunday extension on to

Dartford, by 1939 route 132 had become a circular service linking Eltham Well Hall station, Welling and Bexleyheath. In March 1959, as part of the trolleybus replacement programme, the circular route was discontinued and replaced by a service linking Eltham Well Hall station and Erith. It was revised to run between Eltham and Woolwich from 1964, when operation was reallocated from Sidcup to Bexleyheath.

In 1970 it was revised again to run between Eltham and Slade Green and converted from crew operation with RTs to single-deck SM-class AEC Swifts without conductors. Operation transferred back to Sidcup when Bexleyheath closed in 1986.

Operation of the 86 passed to Boro'line Maidstone in January

1988 following a tendering exercise. In February 1992, Boro'line's London operations were sold to Proudmutual Group, the holding company of Kentish Bus (the former London Country South East), which took over the route.

Retendering in 1998 passed the 89 on to the Belvedere depot of Grays-based Harris Bus, which operated London buses on both sides of the river. Harris Bus went into receivership in December 1999 and after its attempts to find other operators prepared to take on the contracts failed, Transport for London established its own East Thames Buses company, which remained a TfL subsidiary until Go-Ahead purchased it in July 2009.

The route 89 had been extended to North Greenwich station in

January 2009 and in November that year it was reallocated to Bexleyheath garage. In connection with the introduction of night tube services on the Jubilee Line, a 24hr weekend service began in August 2015.

### Extended to a prison

Route 244 was introduced in 1987 to link Woolwich with the newly developed Broadwaters estate at Thamesmead. It was put out to tender soon after becoming part of the Bexleybus operation and passed to London Central in November 1990.

It was extended to Belmarsh Prison the next year, with peak hour journeys running to Thamesmead. In January 1999 it was extended from Belmarsh to Abbey Wood, then in 2004 from Woolwich to the Queen Elizabeth

Hospital. It was reallocated to Belvedere garage, but returned to Bexleyheath from 2 December 2017 when Belvedere closed.

Contracts for London bus routes are awarded for five years and can be extended for a further two years if the operation meets quality performance standards and in exceptional circumstances for longer still. The opening of the Elizabeth Line in stages from December 2018 is likely to change the demand for bus services in the Abbey Wood area, prompting one such exception. To allow time to consult on the proposed changes, which are likely to include double-deckers for route 244, its contract has been extended by a further 12 months.

Today's route 486 has its origins in two services — the M1

and M2 Millennium Transit — introduced to link Millennium Dome at North Greenwich (the O2 arena today) with mainline railway stations at Greenwich and Carlton. The contract to operate them was awarded to London Central, which acquired 17 new DAF SB220 single-deckers with stylish East Lancs Myllennium bodywork, which were allocated to New Cross garage.

The M1 was meant to use a section of guided busway, although this never worked as planned, while three of the buses were fuelled by liquefied petroleum gas rather than diesel. The plan was to withdraw both routes when the dome closed at the end of 2000.

Although the M1 ceased operation on 23 February 2001, North Greenwich station had become a significant interchange point between buses and tubes, so the M2 was instead incorporated into new route 486, which continued beyond Charlton to Welling. In February 2002 it was extended to Bexleyheath along with the 17 DAFs. Double-deckers replaced them when the contract was renewed in 2007.

Route B11 began in January 1988 as part of the Bexleybus scheme. Initially operated by minibuses and branded as the Bexley Hoppa, it linked

**ABOVE: MD15, one of the East Lancs Myllennium-bodied DAF SB220s built for routes M1 and M2, operating route 486 at North Greenwich.**

**LEFT: An Alexander Dennis Enviro200 and a Wright Eclipse Gemini 2-bodied Volvo B9TL over the inspection pits inside the garage.**

Bexleyheath town centre with Lodge Hill, partially replacing a section of route 122. Operation passed to Kentish Bus in 1991 and the route was extended to Abbey Wood station.

Retendering in January 1999 extended the route again, to Thamesmead Boiler House, with a further projection to Thamesmead town centre in 2004 when the route also passed to London Central, thus returning to Bexleyheath Garage. As with the 244, the contract for the B11 has been extended for 12 months pending changes associated with the Elizabeth Line opening. It is likely to be cut back to Abbey Wood station.

The B16 (Kidbrooke-Bexleyheath) was introduced by Bexleybus on 8 July 1989. It replaced a section of route 160 between Eltham and Welling and the B1 between Eltham and Kidbrooke. It has been operated from Bexleyheath for its entire existence.

## Periods of great change

The past 30 years have included some turbulent periods for Bexleyheath garage and its staff and the recent loss of several routes has been unsettling. The Elizabeth Line will likely bring more major change.

A new route 301 linking Bexleyheath with Woolwich is proposed and the tendering

process for this is underway. The 244 and B11 are also being retendered currently. Farther into the future, the Bexley Growth Strategy envisages over 30,000 new homes in the borough by 2050.

The man responsible for leading Bexleyheath garage's 270 staff through this period of change is Jon Verrall, general manager for both Bexleyheath and the former Metrobus operation at Orpington, who joined Go-Ahead in the summer of 2016 after nearly 30 years with Royal Mail. Verrall grew up on the nearby Cray Estate and spent his formative years jumping on and off Routemasters on route 229.

Although he can see many similarities between running buses and delivering mail, one of the differences that struck this

newcomer to the bus industry was the sheer complexity of staff rotas. Instead of blocks of shifts, staff sign on and off constantly.

For most of its trolleybus heyday, Bexley depot (as it was then) had an allocation of around 70 double-deckers. Today, despite recent losses, it still houses over 140 buses including around 20 from Go-Ahead London's commercial services fleet for rail replacement, private hires and other outside work.

They have been moved there in order to be parked under cover, which is particularly important for open-top double-deckers, but also helps preserve the paint finish on heritage Routemasters and other types used at such high profile events as the Chelsea Flower Show and Wimbledon Tennis. ● **ML**

**ABOVE:**
Enviro400s and an Enviro200 inside the bus parking area.

**RIGHT:**
Approaching their last days in service in London, two LDP-class Dennis Dart SLFs with Plaxton Pointer bodies stand on the Bexleyheath garage forecourt.

# Nothing stands still

ABOVE: LT2 — battling heavy traffic around the Wellington Monument — was one of the prototype New Routemasters on the 38 when we featured it in Volume 1, and indeed it was the first of the type to enter public service in February 2012. It is now disguised as a green Country Area London Transport bus — a legacy of being demonstrated in West Yorkshire — and like all other 999 of this type has gained sliding windows to improve ventilation.

## Some of the routes we have followed and featured in previous volumes have seen changes of vehicle types, places served and frequency of operation

In three of the four previous volumes of *The London Bus* we have brought you articles on a total of 17 key London bus routes – services that have a high profile or use especially interesting vehicles.

Each article has provided a snapshot of the route's history, a quick run-down of the bus type or types currently in use on it, our impressions of riding the route and an idea of some of the landmarks you will encounter along the way. You will find five more routes covered in this volume.

However, in the bus world change can come quickly. More than half the routes we have looked at over the past six years have seen alterations of some kind since we prepared our original articles about them. We thought it would be instructive this time to take a look back over what has been happening.

Remarkably, given that Transport for London re-tenders its bus routes every five to seven years, more or less all the routes we have covered have stayed with their original operators so far. You could argue that the 25 is an exception, but it has not changed hands in the usual sense. FirstGroup operated it when we wrote about it in Volume 1, but the company was already in the throes of selling its London operations to Australian-owned Tower Transit. That change went ahead as expected.

The most visible changes have come on routes that have gained new buses. As I write this article in spring of 2018, six of our routes now feature wholly or mainly different buses.

### New Routemasters

Perhaps the most striking change has come on routes that have gained New Routemasters. Chronologically, the first on our list to feature these buses was the high intensity 38 (*Volume 1*) between Victoria station and Clapton in north-east London.

At the time of our article in 2013, Arriva had already put eight early New Routemasters on trial on the route, but the majority of buses were Wright Gemini 2DL integral double-deckers with VDL DB300 running units. Since then, the whole service has been converted to New Routemasters.

The first route that started to receive New Routemasters after

we had written about it was the north-south 24 (*Volume 1*), connecting West Hampstead in north London with the River Thames at Grosvenor Road. In fact this was the first route in London to be converted fully to the new model. When we prepared our article about it in early 2013, operator Metroline was using a mix of Volvo B9TLs and B5LH hybrids, all with smart Wright Gemini 2 bodywork; but the switch to New Routemasters was already planned.

It went ahead at the end of that year, and the 24 became one of an eventual six that actually had conductors or 'attendants' on board (the 38 was another). Then mayor Boris Johnson had promised to revive the facility for

users to board or alight between bus stops, and this would only be permissible if the bus had someone on hand to monitor the doors.

Route 11 (*Volume 1*), which runs across London between Fulham Broadway and Liverpool Street, was another early recipient of New Routemasters, and also had conductors when they first appeared. When we featured the route in 2013, Go-Ahead was using much older Volvo B7TLs with Wright Eclipse Gemini bodywork, but the changeover came in November of that year. It was made mid-contract, but Go-Ahead retained the route when it was re-tendered two years later.

All six of the New Routemaster

routes that once had attendants (the others being the 9, 10 and 390) lost them in 2016, and the hop-on/hop-off facility is now a thing of the past.

## Other changes of type

Not all vehicle updates on the routes we have featured involve New Routemasters. Back in 2013 route 1 (*Volume 1*) between Tottenham Court Road and Canada Water was run by Volvo B7TL double-deckers with classic Wright Eclipse Gemini bodies, along with some Alexander Dennis Enviro400s.

Since late 2016, when the contract with Go-Ahead was renewed, the 1 has been operated by new buses – mostly Volvo B5LH hybrids with Wright Gemini 3 or MCV EvoSeti bodywork.

Go-Ahead is the operator of yet another in our list of routes that has gained new buses – the 14 (*Volume 3*), which runs between Warren Street (Euston) and Putney Common. When we covered it in 2016, the buses were much like those mentioned on other routes above – ageing Volvo B7TLs with Wright Gemini bodywork and similar-looking but much newer Volvo B9TLs with Gemini 2 bodies. Since then the 14 has seen a transformation.

This has come about in response to the low emission bus zones that current London mayor Sadiq Khan started rolling out in March 2017. These focus on 12 London streets deemed to be especially polluted, and one of the first to come into effect was in Putney High Street. Go-Ahead London operates five major double-deck routes through Putney, so it had to upgrade them all at the same time. Four of them are run from its Putney garage – the 14, 22, 74 and 430 – and these now share three new

bus types and one existing type.

New are Alexander Dennis Enviro400 MMCs and Volvo B5LHs, the latter with Wright Gemini 3 and MCV EvoSeti bodies. Retained are older Volvo B5LHs with Wright Eclipse Gemini 2 bodywork. So now you will find as much variety on the 14 as you can ever expect to see on a single London bus route.

The final route in our original list that has seen a change of vehicle type is the 93 (*Volume 4*), an inter-suburban route between Putney Bridge and North Cheam,

which we featured as recently as 2017. Unusually, in this case the buses have changed back to a type that was used before.

The low emission bus zone in Putney is again the culprit. The 93 is another Go-Ahead route, but unlike the other four in the area, it is operated from more distant garages (Sutton and Merton), so could not share in the bounty of new vehicles introduced at Putney. However, it too was using ageing buses: in this case pure diesel Alexander Dennis Enviro400s acquired

nine years before. These were fitted with neatly angular Optare Olympus bodywork – a rare chassis-body combination.

At the time when the low emission zone took effect, the company had already embarked on a refurbishment programme to extend these buses' lives, but it was not very far advanced. A more immediate solution was required, and Go-Ahead's response was to swap the Enviro400s almost overnight with new MCV EvoSeti-bodied Volvo B5LH hybrids from its Peckham garage.

The EvoSetis ran on the 93 for most of 2017, sharing some duties with similar buses fitted with Wright Gemini 3 bodywork; so these were the vehicles we featured in our article. However, behind the scenes the refurbishment programme on the Olympus-bodied Enviro400s continued. They were overhauled, repainted in London's current all-over red livery, and upgraded to the 'clean' specification required for the low emission zone.

Towards the end of 2017 they started to reappear on the 93. Now they're back in large

**LEFT & BELOW: Route 1 still has Wright-bodied Volvos of Go-Ahead London, but Eclipse Gemini-bodied B7TLs like VWL42 new to East Thames Buses in 2004 have given way to Gemini 3-bodied B5LH hybrids like WHV148 passing the Strand Underpass created out of part of the old Kingsway Subway that took trams between the Embankment and Holborn.**

**BELOW: New hybrids like Enviro400H MMC EH96 have ousted older vehicles from route 14.**

**RIGHT & BELOW:**
Also allocated
to route 14
are Wright
Gemini 3-bodied
Volvo B5LHs like
WHV121, which
together with the
Enviro400H MMCs
have replaced
Eclipse Gemini-
bodied Volvo B7TLs
like WVL171.

numbers, and the EvoSetis
have gone, leaving just a few
Gemini 3-bodied Volvos to share
occasional duties with the
Enviro400s. Definitely a case of
back to the future.

## Altered routes and frequencies

After changes in vehicle type,
the most visible alterations in
bus services involve the actual
routes. One of our featured
services, the 3 (*Volume 1*)
between Crystal Palace and
central London, has been
shortened since we wrote
about it.

Back in 2013 it continued
north from Trafalgar Square to
Piccadilly Circus and Regent
Street, terminating at Oxford
Circus. In June 2017 the section
beyond Trafalgar Square was
lopped off.

However, if all goes to plan,
from December 2018 route
3 will gain a new northerly
extension, taking it back up to
Oxford Street via Charing Cross
Road, but now terminating at
its easternmost extremity. It will
then wend its way over to Russell
Square in Bloomsbury, ending up
slightly longer than when Oxford
Circus was the turning point.

Another of our routes has
already been extended. When
we followed the 148 (*Volume
4*) between Camberwell and
Shepherds Bush in 2017, the

north-western terminus was
Shepherds Bush Green. However,
between 2008 and 2015 the
service had continued half a
mile north to White City. Then
that section was withdrawn, but
now that building works on the
old BBC Television Centre and
Westfield shopping centre are
well advanced, the 148 has been

extended again to the adjacent
White City bus station.

Changes in frequency are
perhaps less obvious than
changes in route, though they
will certainly affect regular
users. There have been
reductions in various routes
from our original list, including
the 1, 11, 25 and 205 (*Volume 3*).

To some extent these reductions reflect changes in demand, though in some cases Transport for London had made changes to adjacent routes in order to provide extra capacity.

As an example, when changes were made to the long route 25 from Oxford Street to Ilford (covered in 2013), frequency changes were made at the same time to route 425 between Stratford and Lower Clapton.

As it happens, the future of the central London section of the 25, in common with that of other routes on the same axis, hangs in the balance pending the opening of the east-west Elizabeth Line railway in 2019. If substantial numbers of users switch from bus to rail, that section could be reduced or simply discontinued. ● **PR**

**LEFT:** While they were away from route 93, the DOE-class Enviro400s were loaned to Peckham garage and used on route 63. This was DOE17 at St Pancras station.

**LEFT & BELOW:** The sale of First's London business to Tower Transit saw new company names appear on Wright Eclipse Gemini 2-bodied Volvo B9TLs on route 25 like VN36155 and VN36125.

ABOVE: Nine Routemasters, eight of them in Big Pink Sightseeing livery in support of the Canadian Breast Cancer Foundation, parked on the docks in Saint John, New Brunswick on a day when no cruise ships were calling. PICTURES: ALAN MILLAR

# Routemasters in **Canada**

*The world's largest operator of London Routemasters is neither in London nor anywhere else in the UK, but in Canada's maritime provinces where Absolute Charters has 26 of these iconic London double-deckers used mainly to carry cruise ship passengers on sightseeing tours*

RIGHT: RML2314 at work in Halifax, Nova Scotia with advertising for the Canadian Museum of Immigration. It is calling at Fairview Lawn Cemetery where 121 of the 1,500 victims of the 1912 *Titanic* sinking are buried. This was originally a green Country Area bus and ended its London service with Go-Ahead London General at Putney. It was fitted with a Cummins engine in 1992.

**LEFT: RML2664,** promoting Forest Lakes Country Club with images of happy people relaxing in wooden Adirondack chairs, loading outside the Maritime Museum of the Atlantic in Halifax. Boarding is generally by the additional powered doors fitted in front of the British offside rear wheel. Before entering service at Croydon garage in 1967, it took part in a British Week promotion in Brussels and ended its London career with First CentreWest at Westbourne Park. It was repowered with a Cummins engine in 1990.

**LEFT: RML2336** promoting the Grant Thornton accountancy practice on the streets of Halifax. It was new in 1965 as a Country Area bus at Godstone and ended up with Go-Ahead London Central. It saw subsequent service in Nottingham before being exported. It gained a Cummins engine in 1990.

**RIGHT & BELOW:**
**Rear views of RML2578, which lost original registration JJD 578D before it left the UK, and RML2316, which had a Caterpillar engine fitted when operating for London General in 2002. One advertises Hamachi Asian restaurants, the other a student accommodation service. The original rear platforms are taped off to prevent access. RML2578 began and ended its London life at Putney garage, but saw service in between at Holloway and New Cross. It received a Cummins engine in 1990.**